Establishing Boundaries:

How to Protect Yourself, Become Assertive, Take Back Control, and Set Yourself Free

By Patrick King

Social Interaction and Conversation Coach at www.PatrickKingConsulting.com

Table of Contents

Establishing Boundaries: How to Protect Yourself, Become Assertive, Take Back Control, and Set Yourself Free 2

Table of Contents 4

Chapter One: The Line in the Sand 6
    Drawing the Line 13
    Types of Boundaries 18
    Are You in Need? 26

Chapter Two: Your Relationship with Boundaries 32
    The Conditional Statement 37
    An Important Definition 42
    But where did this come from? 50
    Self-Assessing 61

Chapter Three: Boundaries: The Strong, Weak, Good, and Bad 70
    Finding the Balance 76
    Between a Rock and a Hard Place: Emotional Drain and Loneliness 84
    A Simple Pyramid 90
    It Takes Two to Tango 94

Chapter Four: Knowing Thyself 104
    "I" Statements 111
    You in Relation to Others 114

Recognizing Abuse 120
Your Role, Your Needs 127
The Boundary Habit 138

Chapter Five: Boundaries, Brick by Brick 144
Common Missteps 160
Dealing with Repeat Offenders 167

Chapter Six: It's Not Your Turn 180
Cautiously Prioritizing Others Again 187

Summary Guide 196

Chapter One: The Line in the Sand

Boundaries are one of those things we all take for granted; we never really think about them until they stop working properly. It's easy to see where the limits of our *physical* body are, but where are your psychological, emotional, and even spiritual limits? Do you have a clear idea of where you end and the rest of the world begins? It's common to assume that others will automatically respect the boundaries set between us and them, or that others will simply tell us if we cross their boundaries.

However, creating and maintaining boundaries is a skill, one that most of us haven't expressly been taught. We tend to assume that loose boundaries are good and make us likeable to others, yet we may experience years of poor relationships with others before we even realize that our boundaries are the source of our problems. Similarly, it's easy to mistake overly strict boundaries as a marker of self-respect, but they, too, harm our ability to form healthy bonds with others.

In this book, we'll be looking closely at what a boundary actually is, the different kinds of boundaries that exist, and exactly how to turn unhealthy boundaries into self-serving, nonnegotiable standards. Because it can be so tricky to even recognize a poorly-set boundary, we'll be looking at all the classic signs that one's boundaries could use some work. In addition, we'll also look at the signs and symptoms of insufficient boundaries that are less common.

By digging in deep to uncover the unconscious beliefs that inspire and motivate our everyday behavior, we can begin to unravel the habits that keep us stuck in disrespectful, exhausting, or even abusive dynamics. From there, we can start to build identities that align with the lives we actually want for ourselves. On the surface, boundaries don't seem like such a big deal; however, the closer you look, the more you'll see that mastering the art of perfectly balanced boundaries is at the core of optimum mental, physical, and spiritual health.

The following story is completely fictional, but similar situations have taken place numerous times across the globe. It may have even happened to you—see if you can recognize yourself in it:

A single woman is actively dating and trying out lots of new ways to meet new people. One day, her mother's friend sets her up with a young man who everyone believes she will get along well with. The woman feels awkward and unsure about this, but goes along with it to please her (admittedly nosy) mother. "Just give him a chance," people around her say, and despite feeling uninterested, the woman agrees to the date.

The man turns up at the restaurant at the agreed-upon time and the woman takes an immediate dislike to him. She finds him unattractive, boring, and the complete opposite of the sort of person she is looking for. But despite her discomfort and desire to end the date right then and there, she realizes that she can't bear to look rude or unkind, so she pushes herself to smile and be nice.

She inwardly admonishes herself for being picky, judgmental, and superficial. At the end of the date, she's exhausted and can't wait to get away, but the man suggests that they go get ice cream together. Her heart sinks. He seems so insistent on this outing. Feeling guilty and cornered, she agrees. She says nothing when he touches her arm, and again says nothing when he later tries to hold her hand.

After ice cream, the woman quickly finds herself agreeing to a second date to avoid appearing mean or ungrateful. All the while, what she really wants to say is, "Thanks for your time, but I'm not interested." Won't her mother be disappointed and imply that there's something wrong with her for never being satisfied with anyone?

Won't the man be hurt and feel rejected if she turns him down? Because the woman believes she is heavily responsible for the feelings of everyone else in this scenario, she keeps saying "yes" when she really means "NO."

Date four rolls around and this time, the man invites her over to his place. She doesn't really want to go, but doesn't want to seem prudish, unadventurous, or boring, so she goes anyway.

She holds her tongue when the man says something that she knows is factually incorrect; she accepts drinks when she'd rather not have any; she laughs at jokes she doesn't find funny—after all, she wouldn't want to make him feel uncomfortable, would she?

To conclude, the woman soon feels so *used* that she eventually snaps rudely at the man, then completely avoids him and refuses to answer his calls. He gets angry and wonders why she "led him on." Everyone else involved is incredibly confused—weren't they getting along great? The woman herself has difficulty understanding what happened. He was a nice guy, and she was trying so hard to do the right thing.

So, why did it end so badly?

Let's first consider another example. A woman finds it difficult to progress in her career. She's likeable and good at what she does, but somehow is always overlooked for promotions. One day during a meeting, she notices that her name is misspelled on documents, but keeps quiet—she doesn't want to cause any trouble. Her younger, less-qualified colleague then blatantly suggests her idea to their colleagues, presenting it as his own. She's angry about it, but feels sorry for him and decides to let it slide. She knows just how difficult it can be to make a name for oneself! She decides she doesn't really mind and reassures herself that she can always come up with more ideas.

Later in the meeting, she is asked to take on a task that is not listed in her job description. The task would take significant time and energy that she doesn't have. Unfortunately, she doesn't feel courageous enough or entitled to say "no," and accepts this extra work immediately. On the way home that evening, long after she's supposed to be finished with work, she answers emails on the train and sees an email alerting her that she had been signed up to cater an event at the office that upcoming weekend.

Not only had she not been informed about—or even invited to—this event, it was automatically assumed that she would organize it, simply because she had agreed to do something similar last year. At the end of the year, the woman is asked to train the younger, idea-stealing colleague because they intend to promote him and give him extra responsibilities. Angry and upset, she confronts her boss to ask why *she* was never once considered for the position. His answers stuns her: "You didn't ask."

This woman is a conscientious, hardworking employee who possesses all of the skills and experience needed to succeed in her field. In fact, her department finds her indispensable and leans on her heavily. She knows she's good at what she does, and yet… why does she feel so worthless? Why does she never seem to advance?

Drawing the Line

These women (and men, of course) may have problems with assertiveness or self-esteem, but the bigger issue they have in common is simple: poor boundaries. The first woman knows instantly that she is not interested and doesn't want to continue with her date, but she never feels able to assert this boundary, to confidently say "no" to what she doesn't want, without feeling like a bad person. She decides instead to allow other people to intrude—psychologically, emotionally, even physically—when she would rather have them keep a respectful distance. While she thinks that doing so makes her a "nice" person, the irony is that when she snaps at her date, he is confused and wonders, *Why didn't she just say she wasn't interested in the first place?*

The second woman has a similar problem, although in addition to not being able to say "no," she also seems unable to say yes to what she *does* want. She dutifully martyrs herself by undertaking extra work she is too busy to do, is happy to go without thanks or acknowledgment, and never prioritizes herself, her needs, or her wants. Rather than asking others for help, she takes on extra work for them. Rather than speaking up when she's been hurt, insulted, looked over, or actively violated, she keeps quiet and swallows her anger and disappointment. The result, sadly, is not that people see the many ways she bends over backwards and finally agree that she's worth treating well; instead, they take her for granted even more.

Because she has never stated and defended her boundaries, her colleagues assume that her silence is a tacit agreement to the treatment she gets. If she doesn't care about her needs, limitations, and boundaries, why should they?

In this book, we're going to be looking at what boundaries are, what function they serve, and how difficult life can be when we fail to maintain healthy and appropriate boundaries. It's arguable that women are trained in our society to have weak or non-existent boundaries. However, a part of reclaiming your own space in the world is about taking responsibility and ownership for setting (and respecting!) boundaries—and this applies to both men and women!

A boundary is a line we draw between ourselves and the rest of the world.

Inside of it is who we are, what we want, the meaning we create for ourselves, and more. Outside of it are other people, external events beyond our control, and a reality that is not strictly "our business." Humans are social beings and we're always engaging with others, always negotiating relationships, always sharing and exchanging energies with each other. But through all of this, a healthy person has a crystal clear understanding of *who they are* and the nonnegotiable limits of their being.

A boundary is often assumed to be about keeping something or someone out, but it is much more than this. A boundary acts not only to draw a line around what is *not* you, but also to reinforce and affirm what *is* you. Having strong boundaries doesn't mean you are inflexible, selfish, mean, or uninterested in engaging with others. Rather, knowing and holding boundaries is a beautiful way to celebrate who you are, what you stand for, and all of the things you want to focus on and prioritize in life. A life with established boundaries is one of self-respect—the respect to give yourself what you need and to remove yourself from the things that hurt or degrade you.

Boundaries are about taking mature, proactive responsibility for yourself—never blaming others for your own reality, but at the same time never letting others blame you for theirs. With boundaries, we are in control. We show love to ourselves and to others, because we implicitly communicate that we are valuable. Our time, bodies, emotions, thoughts, beliefs, and actions are valuable. They are worth something—worth being defended and taken care of.

Every time we say "no" to something harmful in the world, we are effectively saying "yes" to ourselves and our own well=being. Every time we say "no" to an intrusive or needy person, we are saying "yes" to them learning their own life lessons without us rescuing them, and "yes" to our own right to autonomous well-being.

A person with intact and healthy boundaries will feel safe, calm, and respected. A person with poor boundaries will feel violated by the world and others, unappreciated, disrespected, overly obliged, guilty, resentful, and insecure. Sadly, sovereignty and self-worth are characteristics that, in our world, need to be fought for. We can strengthen this autonomy, however, by loving ourselves enough to maintain our boundaries.

Types of Boundaries

For people with "boundary issues," the idea of great boundaries seems simple enough, but it can be incredibly challenging to know what exactly that means. Let's start by imagining that there are different kinds of boundaries. You, as a human being, have a selfhood that is autonomous, separate, and with value and worth completely independent of the value you provide others. As a human being, you also possess many different selves: a physical self, an emotional self, and so on.

Physical boundaries affirm that your body belongs to you and nobody else. You can share it with others when you want to, but it is ultimately yours. The most basic right we all have is a right to our own bodies; your physical limits, preferences, and needs are important—as important as anyone else's. Women who have been in abusive relationships can have their physical boundaries eroded over time—they stop believing that their bodies are 100% theirs.

Even a woman who hasn't been abused may buy into the sexist idea that if a man is nice to her and pays for dinner, she "owes" him sex, or that if a partner pushes or intimidates her one day, it's OK because she must deserve it somehow. A physical boundary is also something that we draw to keep out any behaviors, substances, situations, or activities that undermine our body's safety and health.

A physical boundary says: I am here. I belong, and my body is mine and mine alone. I'm allowed to take up space, to say "no," to be tired or sick, to be on my own, to see to my needs. My body is not for others—it's for me.

Emotional boundaries communicate exactly the same thing, but on an emotional level. Your emotions are yours—they can't be wrong or right, and they are not something you should be blamed for or made to feel guilty about. Some people try to control others by controlling their narrative.

They'll say, "Oh, you're being dramatic," or, "You're overreacting." But nobody can tell you what you feel, how you should feel, or what your feelings mean. We're all allowed to feel what we feel. On the other hand, the rights come with responsibilities—we're free to own our own feelings, but not to make others responsible for them or demand that others feel the way we think they should feel.

An emotional boundary says: I feel how I feel. I accept, love, and trust myself. I am the ultimate arbiter over my emotional reality. I know what I feel, and I don't need permission from anybody to feel it.

Mental and spiritual boundaries exist, too. We set up a mental boundary whenever we have the wisdom to say, "That's enough social media for today, it's getting me down. I'm going for a walk instead." Firm mental boundaries allow us to hold opinions or ideas, even when others don't like them, and prevent us from being bullied, coerced, or manipulated away from what we know is best for us.

Spiritual boundaries are similar—with spiritual boundaries, you have the confidence to fully own your spiritual or religious beliefs, and to share them with who you choose to, as much as you choose to. You have the ability to defend and nurture your spirit and soul in just the same way that you'd defend and nurture your body.

Material boundaries involve drawing an empowered line around all of the material possessions we own, most commonly money, but also assets, personal items, clothing, and other belongings. We are not obligated to give and give and give materially, and we don't have to share with others continually to our own detriment. We are allowed to have privacy and to have our own things for our own use.

Mental, spiritual, and material boundaries all say: My life is important. The way I am matters and I'm allowed to pursue what's important to me without feeling guilt or shame.

We can also talk about time boundaries ("I will not spend all of my life working when I have a family I care about!"). Your time is valuable and you have a right to spend it on activities you consider important. Such boundaries are necessary at home and work, as well as in your social relationships. Asking professionals to perform extra work without overtime, being disturbed repeatedly by a friend at inappropriate hours to help solve their problems, and even showing up excessively late are all examples of time boundary violations.

There are sexual boundaries ("I only engage in sexual activities that I want to when I want to, and I deserve to have these boundaries respected"). These are often prone to eroding over time, especially in relationships when partners insist on trying things that you might be uncomfortable with. We can fall into the trap of violating our own boundaries by giving in, but it is important that we respect ourselves enough to stand firm.

Digital boundaries are yet another type of boundary that you might want to consider. This includes discussing with another person whether it is appropriate to use each other's devices, discuss a relationship on social media platforms, share passwords, befriend each other's friends online, etc. This one might require some negotiation and compromise, making communication key in arriving at a workable arrangement.

Finally, energy boundaries are also important in your relationships with others ("I refuse to let myself be drained or depressed by certain people or events"). Some people are naturally more attuned to the positive or negative energies that individuals radiate, and this can have a significant impact on their own mood. If this sounds familiar, try identifying the types of situations or people that act as triggers. Distance yourself from these triggers.

You might find spending time with a particular family member bothersome, yet worry about appearing rude for avoiding them. In such cases, you must prioritize self-care over social norms. It's hard to imagine either woman in our examples thinking or believing any of the above.

So, why do people like these women have poor boundaries in the first place? The answer is complex, and we'll explore cultural, familial, and historical reasons in more detail later. Whatever the reason for it, a poor boundary is an external manifestation of an internal reality. Ultimately, poor boundaries likely accompany any *set of beliefs* that tells us that we are less important than others.

We might tell ourselves:

- I can't be bothered to say something.
- I don't want to cause any drama.
- People might dislike me if I'm not exactly how they want me to be.
- I don't have a right to demand more.
- I might be punished if I am too assertive.
- I hate being "aggressive."
- People who set boundaries are mean and selfish, and I don't want others to think that of me.
- I'm only a "good" person if I help others feel better somehow.
- I'm not entitled to be happy.
- Other people's wants are more legitimate and important than my own.

For now, it's enough to know that a boundary is something we draw around our *valuable and distinctive selves*, in accordance with our needs and values. Many of us lack boundaries simply because we falsely believe that we don't deserve them.

A boundary can look like a tolerance ("I will end a relationship with anyone who tries to control or manipulate me"), a limit ("I will not work on the weekends"), or an expectation ("I expect my family to treat me with respect"), but they all communicate a nonnegotiable degree of value you place on yourself and the minimal conditions for interacting with you.

In later chapters, we'll consider exactly *how* to discover your boundaries, as well as how to enforce them, but for now, consider that boundaries are all unique to the person who makes them. There are no wrong or unreasonable boundaries, and you are free to create any boundaries you want.

Are You in Need?

If you've had the misfortune to receive messages from others stating that your needs are less important than theirs, you may find it difficult not only to know what your boundaries are, but also to convincingly communicate them. Oftentimes, we internalize these messages after being exposed to them over a long period of time, through different people who all seem to agree on our (low) worth. We may fear offending people, damaging relationships, or coming across as mean or selfish.

However, with practice, we can all learn (and *must* learn!) how to assert boundaries without aggression or guilt.

The most important work is to truly understand your own worth and *believe in it* before trying to convince someone else of it. Much advice you'll see about setting boundaries focuses only on superficial changes, such as what specifically to say or do. But meekly saying "no" in a quiet voice with body language that suggests you don't expect to be taken seriously will seldom work. To be calm and self-assured, to hold yourself with dignity, to speak confidently and clearly—these things are not possible without a genuine shift in the way you view yourself and the world.

In the chapters that remain, we'll go a little deeper and explore not only the practical aspects of maintaining boundaries, but also what it means to have the self-worth and self-respect from which healthy boundaries emanate. Many of us have had poor early childhood experiences around needs, rights, and self-worth—but we can always learn!

By the time you've read this book, you should feel more comfortable and at home in your own value, able to identify your needs and limits, and know precisely how to communicate them to others in your life. You'll learn to have better and more empowered relationships with others, but more than this, you will learn to feel more autonomous and secure within *yourself*.

The topic of boundaries is a deceptively simple one—though we can all grasp the concept intellectually, it takes immense self-knowledge and courage to practice the principles that inform truly healthy boundary-setting. Anybody can simply copy the behaviors of balanced, self-assured people, but readers of this book can expect to delve a little deeper and start to cultivate that strong sense of awareness, self-worth, and respect that makes good boundaries a natural and inevitable behavior.

We'll look at many of the theories and models behind boundaries, but focus also on practical, real-world ways that you can start claiming and asserting your own boundaries, right now.

At the end of this book, you'll be able to see clearly why the women in our opening examples experienced what they did, and how they could have done things differently—i.e., in a way that honored and respected their needs and limits. You'll also start developing your own mental toolkit to help you better understand what you need for your well-being and exactly how to calmly ask for it from the world, confident in the expectation that your experience matters and deserves to be respected.

Unhealthy boundaries take a lifetime to develop; replacing them with better ones won't happen overnight. But with some self-compassion, awareness, and an unshaken belief in your own worth as the marvelously unique human being that you are, you can begin to set up exactly those conditions in life that will most serve your happiness and success.

The process will undoubtedly involve much trial and error, but with enough persistence, you will eventually be successful at not only projecting a confident, self-assured personality, but also feeling the part yourself.

Takeaways

- A boundary is a line between us as individuals and the rest of the world. Inside of this boundary lies everything related to ourselves, things that are relevant to us and that are under our control. Outside of it is everything else.
- In our social interactions, our boundaries define what we are

comfortable with, based on our values and conceptions of what is important and what isn't. Having healthy boundaries is a key component of good relationships and friendships.

- It is common for people to have poor boundaries due to the cultural messages or upbringing that they have experienced. We are repeatedly told to avoid saying "no" in our lives, to quietly accept any mistreatment from others so as to not bother anyone else. However, poor boundaries result in low self-esteem, a sense of being out of control of your life, and resentment towards others. It also leads to us being subjected to exploitative behavior from those who are all too happy to use our poor boundaries to their advantage.
- There are several different types of boundaries that one can have. These include physical, emotional, spiritual, sexual, digital, time, and even energy boundaries. All of these various categories, however, reinforce the

same message—that you are important and deserve to be respected. Whether this is with respect to your body, your feelings, your time, your sexual preferences, or something else, you have a right to demand what you desire in an appropriate manner.
- This book and the following chapters are for those who, for one reason or another, have come to develop boundaries that are either too loose or too rigid. This requires not only being familiar with what exactly healthy boundaries are, but also a fundamental shift in how you view yourself. Others will believe in your worth only once you yourself do, and this book aims to cultivate a positive self-image in its readers.

Chapter Two: Your Relationship with Boundaries

A personal boundary is a rule or limit we set up to moderate our interactions with others and the outside world. It's a conditional statement that lets us decide whether something is acceptable or unacceptable to us. A violated boundary is a signal to us to protect ourselves when necessary.

There are two ways this process can go wrong: having overly rigid boundaries means that you shut people out and deny yourself intimacy; but on the other hand, boundaries that are too permeable can be just as bad. The balance is somewhere right in the middle—a healthy boundary.

How do you know where your boundaries fall? Well, that's the joy of boundaries. Nobody can (or should) answer this question but you! You get to decide your own preferences of engagement with people—and you can change your mind at any time. That being said, there are some telltale clues that your boundaries are not really working for you. All boundaries are *permitted*, but not all of them are *beneficial*. Your boundaries may be considered a little too rigid if you:

- Avoid intimacy in general
- Dislike asking for help
- Try hard to avoid rejection or criticism
- Feel lonely
- Keep people at arm's length
- Seldom compromise
- Feel detached, protective or extremely private
- Have few close relationships

On the other hand, your boundaries may be too porous if you:

- Often find yourself settling for disrespect or outright abuse
- Never speak up for yourself
- Feel dependent on others and their approval
- Have trouble saying "no"
- Overshare the details of your life
- Are deeply sensitive to and aware of other people's emotions, sometimes making those emotions your personal responsibility
- Find it hard to make a decision on your own, and are not confident in your own judgment
- Have relationships that are dramatic, difficult, or codependent
- Frequently feel manipulated, bullied, taken advantage of, dominated, controlled, pushed, violated, pressured, used...
- Sometimes resort to passive aggression to get what you want
- Feel that you're not really sure who you are, deep down

- Regularly feel guilty, anxious, overcommitted, or resentful at others' demands
- Feel very responsible for others' happiness
- Constantly feel like you put more into every relationship than you get out
- Feel run-down and depleted of energy often
- Feel like the victim a lot of the time
- Are deeply fearful of being abandoned or judged as a bad person

If you're reading these lists and see some of yourself in *both*, that's understandable—humans are complex and may have boundaries that are too weak one moment and too strong the next, almost to overcompensate. Alternatively, we may find ourselves relatively stern and self-contained in one aspect of life (for example, work) but it's a completely different story in another area of life (say, romantic relationships).

Whether they're too strong or too weak, unhealthy boundaries have a predictable effect on us: they interfere with our ability to connect healthily and meaningfully with those around us. Intimacy is something to negotiate—and a poor boundary fails to find a balance.

Those with overly strong boundaries may feel they are protecting themselves by being "independent," just as those with porous boundaries may feel they are being good, kind people. But ultimately, our healthiest relationships occur when we can seek intimacy while still maintaining a robust sense of our own autonomy.

You'll know your boundaries are in good shape when you can say *and* hear "no" without feeling bad. When you can value your thoughts, opinions, and feelings, as well as consider those of others. When you feel confident enough to never have to change who you are in order to be approved of by others, but are mature enough to compromise when needed. Most importantly, whatever you do is because you consciously *choose* to do it, according to your own values.

We've already considered the different types of boundaries, but we'll be focusing in this book primarily on those that are usually the most challenging—interpersonal and emotional boundaries with others. In any case, all boundaries are strongly linked to one another. For example, poor emotional boundaries can leak into all areas of life, including our work, our sexual relationships, or our daily habits.

The Conditional Statement

Later in the book, we will spend a little more time on considering how boundaries can be not only set up, but *enforced*. The important thing about a boundary is that it actually means something. It's essentially a conditional statement saying, "If this happens, this is what I will do." It only has power as long as you and everyone else believes you will act on it.

A boundary with no real-world consequences for violation is simply no boundary at all.

Let's consider an example. A very basic physical boundary of yours might be that you dislike being hugged by strangers. To enforce this boundary, you could keep your distance from others, politely decline hugs, or kindly explain to people that you generally avoid hugs. You could consider what would actually happen if this boundary was violated—what would you do? Would your response be effective?

By outlining all of these potential scenarios, you take control of your own desires, limits, and personal space. You turn your beliefs about yourself into concrete action that has a real effect on others. It can be hard in the moment, for example, to let someone know you are uncomfortable with how close they are standing to you, but if you spend the time to figure out a polite way to voice your boundaries beforehand, you can feel more empowered in social situations to simply say what you feel without feeling uncomfortable. The inner work informs the outer work.

No matter how big or small your needs seem, it's important to take the time to understand what *you* want and are comfortable with. But this is only half of the story. It's also necessary to know how you'll respond when and if people don't respect these boundaries. Your reaction to the violation of different boundaries is sure to vary, and you'll need to think of how severe of a reaction each violation deserves. This is where the real power comes in—you teach others to respect and be considerate of you when you communicate that your boundaries are nonnegotiable and that you mean them.

It can feel scary at first to assert a boundary, but it only becomes easier with time, and your confidence can only grow.

As you learn to define and defend your boundaries, you may learn something interesting—that there are genuinely good people out there who are happy to respect them. On the other hand, some of your closest friends and acquaintances will stubbornly continue to treat you in disrespectful ways. Acknowledge this and be mindful of those people who make you feel guilty or punish you for not being as they'd like.

What are *they* communicating when they fail to respect a boundary set up to protect you? Do you agree with that message? This might be a useful indicator of an overly harsh boundary in some cases, but the fact that they chose to violate your boundaries instead of communicating clearly with you is also telling.

It can be a vicious cycle—when we are disrespected, we may internalize the belief that we are not worth much, and then conduct ourselves in a way that courts and allows further disrespect. But we can turn this cycle the other way around. The more we say what we want and need, and the more we act to align with that, the more we shape a life that supports our well-being, filled with people who respect and care for us.

That might take the form of saying "no" to sexual activity that we feel goes against our spiritual beliefs.

It might mean politely telling your bosses that it's not your job to fetch coffee for them.

It may look like you firmly making your purse or handbag off limits to your children, and following up with consequences when this boundary is violated.

It may be the realization that in your relationship, you are sick of being the one to do 90% of the work.

It may mean telling your super extroverted friend that you cannot go out with them for the third night this week because you're tired, you're cranky, and your bank account is suffering!

A wonderful thing happens when we sharpen up and reinforce our boundaries. It's as though our identities come into clearer focus, and we feel more empowered and certain in who we are. We can look life straight in the eyes and say, "This is who I am and what I stand for. I don't have to be any way I don't want to. I'm valuable and there are right and wrong ways to treat me."

A boundary is an idea of self-worth put into practice. Working on better boundaries can be a slow process, but it's a positive feedback loop. The more you affirm and value who you are as an individual, the stronger you'll feel, and the more clarity you'll have on exactly how you want to live your life. Because it is, after all, *your life*.

An Important Definition

It's Christmas day and a little girl is told to kiss her grandmother on the cheek and wish her a Merry Christmas. The girl is shy and turns her face away, saying she doesn't want to. The mother admonishes her: "Don't be mean to granny! Go on, give her a kiss!" and pushes the child towards her grandmother.

What lesson is learnt here? In this all-too-normal occurrence, we see the seeds of poor boundaries being sown. Every human being undergoes a period of socialization in life. We all need to learn to respect ourselves and others, to give and take, to talk and listen. But often, the balance isn't quite right, and we can carry incredibly damaging beliefs about ourselves from childhood into adulthood.

Many people will barely spend any time figuring out exactly what their boundaries are. They assume that each context or situation will tell them how to behave, or they simply default to the dominant cultural or relational messages they've adopted purely by habit. But how well do you really know yourself and what you need? Have you ever really taken the time to outline your own set of core personal beliefs, needs, individual perspectives, wants, limits, and values?

Boundaries are not just for people leaving abusive relationships. They're for *everyone*.

They're important because they help you say "no," calmly and confidently. They let you live an empowered life that you feel in control of. They attract respectful, caring people into your world and allow you to have deeper, more mature connections with them.

You'll have more physical, emotional, and spiritual energy, you'll speak up when wronged, and you'll feel more valued and appreciated in life. You'll understand your needs and therefore have a greater chance of fulfilling them. You'll be emotionally balanced, self-aware, and have rock-solid self-esteem that gives you the courage to be exactly who you are to your fullest potential.

Shouldn't all of that put healthy personal boundaries at the top of your priorities list?

Many people who were socialized as children to be "nice" have developed the idea that having boundaries and a sense of self-respect is "not nice;" that good people always say "yes" and never put themselves before others. Isn't this crazy? Fortunately, choosing whether to set boundaries is not a choice between being a doormat or being selfish. These misconceptions speak to a fundamental misunderstanding of what boundaries are. Before we continue, let's address some of these ideas now to dispel any myths and assure you that developing healthy boundaries will not transform you into a bad or selfish person!

1. Boundaries are not selfish

It's OK to value your own personal well-being and to protect yourself—you are valuable and deserve respect! You are not obligated to serve others in order to have worth—you have it already, and certainly do not lose any when you fail to bend to others' demands, especially if those demands are unhealthy for you. Setting boundaries is an act of self-love, not of selfishness. Think of someone you love—wouldn't you want them to behave in a way that respects their value?

If your best friend comes to you saying that their significant other has been mistreating them in some way, what do you think you would advise them to do? Would you advise them to continue tolerating unacceptable behavior, or would you encourage them to communicate their feelings and try to ameliorate the situation? The answer is most likely the former, and we must apply the same principles in our own lives.

It is not uncommon to be accused of selfishness when you begin to take the way you're treated seriously. You might be surprised by the people who choose to undermine this positive step in your life, but it is imperative that you stay firm on what you consider nonnegotiable. This will help you not only to build confidence and self-esteem, but also to attract other individuals who respect you for choosing to maintain healthy boundaries.

2. Boundaries are not about shutting down intimacy

Boundaries related to intimacy tend to be either extremely rigid or overly lax, especially in romantic relationships. Some of us believe that our partners "deserve" intimacy, even at our own expense. You might be worried that drawing a line in the sand means that people can't be close anymore, that you are somehow being cold or aloof. You needn't worry—people with healthy boundaries have them because they are a prerequisite for healthy, mature relationships. They lead to better relationships, not worse ones. Would you rather have a relationship based on guilt, fear, obligation, and coercion, or one built around mature trust, respect, joy, and appreciation for one another?

Having said that, it is easy to use boundaries to shut down intimacy. Say you're someone who refuses to engage in any form of sex before marriage. Are you using boundaries to shut down intimacy? The truthful answer is that it depends. You might be in what can be called a 'defended state,' wherein you shut out any and all intimate interaction due to past trauma.

Or, you might be enforcing such a boundary due to religious or moral beliefs. It is easy to mistake a defended state for a genuine boundary. Regardless of why you refrain from intercourse, you are within your rights to do so if it brings you discomfort. Yet, the former is almost certainly psychologically unhealthy, as it closes you off from new experiences.

In such cases, it is helpful to ask yourself why you choose to set up and defend a particular boundary. Are you genuinely uncomfortable with being intimate in certain ways, or are you trying to protect yourself from pain due to past experiences?

3. Boundaries won't make you unlikable

Here, we encounter more of the unfortunate social conditioning that women typically receive, even as little children. Everyone wants to be liked. But that sense of belonging and approval should never come at the cost of your well-being. Compromising your own values or hurting yourself in order to acquiesce to someone else's needs doesn't make you likeable—it makes you usable. In fact, a person who has boundaries is sending a powerful message to the world. That message is, "I have value, and I behave accordingly." That is an attractive, healthy, and admirable quality. And it's also true! Most healthy people will be drawn to an attitude of mature, calm confidence.

And the people who do dislike you for setting up a boundary? They are not the sort of people you want to impress. These are the kinds of people who will not see you as the valuable and unique human you are. They will only see you as a tool, as a means to get what they want. Do you *really* want to appeal to such a person?

4. Boundaries are not about who is right and who is wrong

That said, a person with healthy boundaries needs never divide the world into sinners and saints. It makes little difference if there are narcissists or "energy vampires" out there. All that matters is that *you* know who you are, what you want, and what you will tolerate, and that you need never willingly be in a situation that doesn't serve you. This attitude also removes any question of who is right and wrong.

A boundary can never be wrong. This means that you don't have to justify or defend or explain it to others—if it works for you, it works for you. Don't worry about doing it right. You don't need to rigidly think of the world in black and white terms, or be pressured to adopt boundaries in a way that you don't genuinely resonate with. If you're ever unsure, come back to yourself—ask how you feel and what you value. Then, go from there. And remember, there's no rule that says you can't change your mind! Nothing is set in stone, so don't take things super-seriously and beat yourself up if it takes some trial and error.

You are bound to make mistakes, especially at the beginning, as you go about enforcing your boundaries. As long as you're respectful and polite but firm, allow yourself any unintentional errors.

But where did this come from?

When we first come into the world, we have no boundaries. But we come into a world full of other people and *their* boundaries. Think about what this means.

For the first nine months of life we are literally inside of another person, our mother, and for many years after that the boundaries of our ego and hers are loose and undefined. As we grow up and learn who we are as individual human beings, we gradually take on the work of setting up an identity with boundaries. Of deciding who we are and who we aren't, what we do and what we don't. In figuring out *who we are*, we simultaneously figure out how we want the world to treat us.

It's understandable, then, that poor boundaries stem from childhood, during that delicate stage where we are still learning about our value, our autonomy, and our right to draw a line around ourselves. You may take the stance that not everything must come from our childhoods, dismissing that as entirely too Freudian or psychological. But if you're struggling with a belief, conscious or subconscious, chances are it goes back to your youth and the influences of that time.

It's tempting to look at a rotten childhood and blame ourselves or others, concluding that nothing can be done. But as with all trauma, it's not our fault that it happened, but it is our responsibility to do what we can to heal. As adults, we can seek to correct some of the faulty messages we received as children, and do better going forward.

Children depend on their caregivers for survival. Poor boundaries often come from learning to do whatever it takes to survive, even if it's compromising your own selfhood, autonomy, or dignity. You may have also grown up seeing others with poor boundaries, and simply never learnt what a healthy one looks like. You may even be guilty of failing to respect the boundaries of others.

Our parents teach us what is acceptable. What did you learn from them?

Our parents also teach us how valuable we are—what messages did you internalize?

Your parents may have sent you the unconscious message: "We will only love you when you behave exactly as we want you to," or, "Your needs are not as important as mine or your sibling's," or even, "You don't deserve to get your needs met, your job is only to meet the needs of others." This kind of treatment is all too common because historically, most cultures have valorized self-sacrifice and martyrdom in the interest of the greater good.

Those who had to parent their parents, those who felt extreme pressure to conform or perform, and those who were taught that self-sacrifice is good and speaking up is bad—they all might develop poor boundaries.

As we saw in the example of the little girl and her grandmother, this isn't always as sinister as it sounds. Sometimes, our culture's broad messages confirm unhealthy boundaries. We praise the employee who works overtime and neglects their family, and judge the person who cancels plans because they're tired.

Some people have poor boundaries because of more serious trauma in early life. A child whose worth and autonomy are protected in childhood will grow up feeling safe and secure in their own identity. But a child who hasn't had their needs met, or who experienced any kind of abuse or neglect, has experienced the most fundamental boundary violation.

Children who don't have control over their own bodies, personal space, emotions, or behavior may understandably feel confused and worthless, maybe even learning that they don't deserve to fight for or demand better treatment. Such a child may grow into an adult who doesn't even believe that they have a right to themselves, to say "no," to want what they want. This can easily lead to a host of mental health problems, substance abuse, poor relationships, and more.

What is damaged is the personal sense of worth, individuality, dignity, and autonomy. It might not be clear to a person who has suffered abuse that they even have a problem—they don't know what boundaries are, or how to set them. Rather than identifying the source of their pain as external, they may blame themselves, feeling that they are worthless or that they deserve any bad treatment they receive or despair they feel.

Again, this isn't to say that experiencing abuse necessarily means you have poor boundaries, or that you can't have poor boundaries unless you've experienced some horrible trauma in your early life. Because so many factors go into the shaping and maintenance of our identities, unhealthy boundaries are likely the result of many overlapping causes. Your immediate upbringing counts, but so does your culture and what it tells you about appropriate behavior, your life experiences, your previous relationships of all kinds, your unique personality, your worldview and how you envision yourself in the middle of that world, your values, your expectations, your age, your gender, and so on.

An interesting thing to remember is that we are all connected to other people *who themselves have their own boundaries* (or boundary issues, as it were). When you consider the fact that each of us grows up in a home environment consisting of several different people, each with their own boundaries, and their own impact on us, we can see how complex of an issue this really is.

A parent who routinely violates or negates our right to have boundaries may cause us to grow up with a correspondingly weaker, more permeable sense of self.

Families are like ecosystems—because we are interdependent, our behavior and attitudes can't help but affect others around us. Though modern psychology always seems to suggest that individuals are the fundamental unit, the reality is that who we are is very much shaped by how others behave around us. If these people are our primary caregivers during our formative years, this is even more true.

Within families, boundaries serve to separate individuals, but they also work to define ways in which people are linked together and the nature of their relationships. The definition is mutual and reciprocal—there is no child without a mother, no aggressor without a victim. Boundaries within families can also establish smaller walls around subgroups, or a big barrier separating "us" from "them."

Boundaries can decide who's in or out, who's one of us and who isn't, who is good and who is bad.

We've seen that overly rigid or overly permeable barriers can be problematic. Boundary issues are often a family affair—something that affects everyone—and problematic boundaries often come in complementary, dysfunctional pairs. Overly intrusive boundaries can lead to enmeshment, and overly rigid ones can lead to neglect or a sense of emotional detachment. Some examples of the results of poor boundaries include:

- Smothering children and giving them no privacy

- Parents who overly sexualize their children, or make inappropriate demands of them, as in cases where the child and parent role are reversed
- Parents who use their children as confidantes, informal therapists or emotional punching bags
- Parents who involve their children in adult fights, or else make them messengers or bargaining chips in divorce proceedings
- Parents or siblings who snoop, overshare or demand to be a part of other family members' private lives

The examples above are where boundaries are weak or too porous. People suffer from not being properly separated and defined apart from one another—they become enmeshed. On the other hand, boundaries that are too rigid result in a family that is distant and detached from one another.

In one family, there may be *both* detachment and enmeshment at once; for example, parents may be very intrusive with their children and frequently violate emotional, mental, or social boundaries, but be relatively detached when it comes to physical boundaries, i.e. rarely showing physical affection like hugging and allowing the children to have their own private rooms and possessions.

It's not too hard to see how this particular pattern of boundary dysfunction might shape the personalities and attitudes of the children growing up.

Overly rigid boundaries may show up as:

- Parents who withhold information and treat their children with coldness or aloofness
- Parents who fail to provide a safe, loving, and stable environment or neglect their children
- It may be an open secret that one of the parents is having an affair, resulting in the children feeling like the boundary around the family unit has been violated
- Parents may make plans that don't involve children or other members of

the family, giving them no say about the plans at all

- Family members may treat one another formally, as competitors or with neutral detachment, never asking for or offering help

We can see that by understanding our family history and dynamics, we understand how unhealthy boundaries originate from the very beginning. The work of building healthy boundaries is the work of undoing old beliefs and starting again with new, healthier ones. By understanding not just *yourself* and how you function, but also how your personality connects to and is informed by a more complex family system, you can begin to make changes.

But what if you truly don't think that your family of origin played a significant role in the difficulties you experience with boundaries? Could it be that other factors have played a bigger role? Healthy boundaries can slowly be eroded with bad experiences or gradually morph into unhealthy ones, given our relationship history with others. Abusive, coercive, controlling, or disrespectful work, platonic, or romantic relationships can cause enormous damage, wearing away our self-belief and sense of worth.

Some people find that it takes time to recover from such painful dynamics, since they need to carefully "recalibrate," remind themselves of their value again, and try to re-establish boundaries that will support their well-being.

Finally, boundaries are not always black and white: we can have largely healthy boundaries that may still have a few weak points, or have moments where we occasionally need to "refresh" or tighten up boundaries as part of our routine self-care. It never hurts to bring more conscious awareness to how we hold our own boundaries.

What's more, it's not work we do once and then never again, but rather something that continues throughout life. Crises or challenging experiences may force us to reconsider old beliefs, and changes in life circumstances may need us to try out a completely new set of boundaries.

Self-Assessing

As you can imagine, it's a little tricky sometimes to *know* if you have poor boundaries or not. Many women, for example, remain in abusive and unhealthy relationships because they doubt their own assessment of the situation. Her partner (as a part of him violating her boundaries) will tell her that she is being unreasonable, that she is imagining things, that she deserves what she gets, or even that *she* is the one who is the boundary-violator.

Similarly, a domineering family member or boss can use guilt tactics, shame, or fear to conceal the fact that they are repeatedly disregarding or trampling over boundaries. Most heartbreaking of all, when children have their boundaries broken, they may grow up sincerely believing they don't have the right to ask for better; they expect that promises will never be kept, that people can't be trusted, or that others have the right to decide what is appropriate for them.

Many people have a mistaken idea of what a healthy boundary looks like—they may recognize that something isn't right, but attempt to fix it with a boundary that is *still* unhealthy, only in a different way. A mother may decide that her kids treat her like a doormat and mistakenly think that the only way to regain control is to be harsh or uncaring to her children, or cut them out of her life completely.

A man might decide that he's tired of being taken advantage of and hurt in dating, and retaliate by preemptively taking advantage of others. Many of us may think that a poor boundary can be corrected with aggression, coldness, ultra-independence or even a fearful victim mentality where the entire world is out to persecute us. But this will not fix the underlying problem.

A good way to start working with boundaries is to bear in mind the fact that as mature adults, *we are always responsible for setting up and enforcing our boundaries*. We cannot force others to do what they don't want to—including treat us well—but we can decide how *we* will behave if we encounter poor treatment. We cannot tell others what they should value or how they should behave, but we can affirm what we value and what we will do. In fact, it is both a right and a responsibility to have functioning boundaries.

Sometimes, it is tempting to retain a victim mindset that says that you are helpless about the bad things happening to you, that you can't really change the circumstances that cause them. This allows us to blame others and engage is self-pity, but it is neither true nor healthy. We are in control of how others treat us, and the best way to change that is by setting an example and treating yourself well.

Your feelings will help you find the middle road between boundaries that are too harsh or too loose. To check on the state of your boundaries, it is necessary only to listen to your intuition, and to respect and acknowledge what you hear. The following are some lesser-known signs that poor boundaries are an unacknowledged problem area for you. See if you notice any of the following feelings or attitudes showing up in your own life:

- You feel unsure of yourself and not much of an individual. When you ask yourself what you want, you often can only think of what others want. It feels like you never really get to be your unique self.
- You feel numb and like you've given up. You often tell yourself that what you feel doesn't matter, anyway, and it's easier just to go along with others.
- You feel like a complete victim or even a martyr—but you also wonder why being such a good person is never rewarded!
- You feel invisible, like half a person or smaller, and less important than others.
- Sometimes you feel cold and detached, never expecting anything good, perhaps in an attempt to protect yourself or downplay how much you hurt.

- You feel on edge, watched, like you have no private business of your own, and that everyone is constantly involved in your life.
- You feel strangled and smothered by other people and their desires, problems, opinions.
- You sometimes find yourself revealing very personal information to a person you don't really know that well.
- You feel like you fall in love easily and act easily on sexual impulse.
- You find it hard to tell when people are being inappropriate, or when you're being lied to or taken advantage of.
- You often feel like you should take whatever you're given and be grateful, rather than take time to decide if it's really what you want.
- You often feel like other people are in the driving seat and you are the passenger—you let others direct your life or describe and define it. You may even feel like others know

you better than you know yourself and can anticipate your needs.
- You expect others to fill your needs automatically or even fantasize that someone may swoop in to take care of you completely.
- You feel like you could sometimes give indefinitely, with no limit, or that you would not stop others from continuously taking from you until nothing was left.
- You have issues with low self-esteem; abuse of food, substances, or sex; or self-harming behaviors.
- You're often unsure what you think or feel about something until you can talk to others about it.

Any time you feel coerced, pressured, intruded upon, smothered, or as though someone or something is coming in too close, it's a good indication that a boundary has been violated. If you generally find that you have difficulty identifying your own wants, values, limitations, or goals, then you may have long-term problems with healthy boundaries.

The first step in setting better boundaries is to *trust yourself to do it*. It may take a little trial and error, and certain people in your life may not like it, but the more you practice, the clearer your own internal signals and intuition will become, and the easier it will be for you to say, "No. That's not me and I don't want that." You might also want to consider seeking professional help. In the case of long-term problems, a therapist can help you navigate through the issues you're facing in an efficient manner.

This will save you much time and heartache as compared to attempting this alone, and we can all use some help with being mentally and emotionally healthier individuals.

Takeaways

- Personal boundaries are limits we place for ourselves and others in our interactions with others. They define the kinds of behavior that we are both comfortable and not comfortable with. However, the process of setting up boundaries can go awry if we choose boundaries that are either too harsh or too permeable. For instance, rejecting intimacy altogether is a sign of the former, while being too afraid to speak up for yourself is an example of the latter.

- Asserting your boundaries can be a frightening and scary prospect, especially for those of us who have never done so before. We may be afraid of conflict, or terrified at the possibility of being disliked by others who might not agree with our boundaries. Despite the initial reluctance, it is nevertheless crucial for us to express and communicate with others things that are not acceptable to us. This helps us to develop a positive self-esteem and attract healthy relationships in our lives.
- We tend to think that boundaries make us selfish, that we won't be well-liked by others if we enforce

them, or that it is somehow overly demanding of others. None of these are true. Learning how to create and maintain boundaries is an important skill that is useful for everyone.
- There are many different reasons why so many of us have poor boundaries to begin with. One of the most common ones is suffering from childhood trauma, as this is where beliefs are formulated and solidified, for better or worse. Children who did not feel safe growing up or had their boundaries routinely violated are bound to internalize the lack of self-worth that others have projected onto them. Our cultures in general also tend to valorize sacrifice and martyrdom at the expense of personal happiness. Though we may have been disadvantaged in terms of learning about boundaries, it is nevertheless important to recognize that enforcing and communicating boundaries is solely our responsibility.

Chapter Three: Boundaries: The Strong, Weak, Good, and Bad

Let's return for a moment to the two women we began our book with. Do you remember the woman who allowed herself to be coerced into dating a man she wasn't interested in, only to cause offense when she found herself in a corner, almost needing to be rude to him to reassert he boundaries after having them violated little by little? You can probably understand her actions a little better now, knowing how and why boundary issues develop.

Let's imagine this woman has had enough and starts to work on trusting herself and her own limits and desires for her own life. She has a word with her mother and politely and gently tells her to butt out of her love life. She spends time with a therapist to figure out what *she* wants from life—and what she doesn't.

Knowing she has to tighten up her boundaries and become more discerning, she approaches dating completely differently. First, she decides she wants to be single for an entire year first, to find herself before dating again. After this, she decides very carefully on the kind of relationship she wants, and tells herself in no uncertain terms that she will not entertain anything that doesn't fit her criteria.

She shuts down men that flirt with her, and goes on countless dates that she cuts short in the middle, telling people directly that she is uninterested. She communicates loudly and clearly: she wants to be married and have kids within two years, she is unwilling to have sex before marriage, and she has a laundry list of qualities her ideal mate must fill—some of them very unreasonable.

One day, a great match comes along. She confidently asserts on the first date that she will not kiss, hug, or touch this man until they've been together for at least 3 months. She even makes a suggestion that she is more moral and better developed as a person than he is because of her attitude. Bewildered, the man gently teases her and asks if there are any exceptions if they really get on well (which they do). The woman is enraged at this boundary violation. She never contacts him again.

You can see what's happened: she has "corrected" her previous poor boundaries with yet more poor boundaries! In fact, the woman has developed such rigid boundaries that she has even started to violate the boundaries of others—when she shames her date without knowing much about him simply because he's not behaving in the way that she wants him to, she's venturing into inappropriate territory herself.

Though it's true that we are free to set any boundary we like, there are a few clues that these are "bad" boundaries—they are not serving the woman's own best interest, and may even violate the boundaries of others. In sex and relationships, it's true that our own comfort, desires, values, and unique personalities are paramount.

But whenever we engage with others, *their* boundaries come into play, too. Though we all have a fundamental right to our own limits, we also exist in a cultural and familial context. In these broader systems, our behavior is not 100% determined by us, but also by consensus reality and the cultural norms that we live inside of.

It's arguable that this woman's behavior may have worked in a completely different culture or historical period, but the fact is that she will only disadvantage herself by having such rigid boundaries. Her date will understandably decide that he can't devote years of his life courting a woman so determined to avoid intimacy.

When people say "boundary issues," they usually mean that the line drawn around someone's identity is too permeable. But we've already seen that a lack of permeability is just as big a problem. The goal is not simply to ramp up assertiveness, confidence, and independence—sometimes, a simultaneous effort to be vulnerable, open, and accommodating *in the right ways* is necessary.

Many people escaping abusive homes or relationships find it relatively easy to get rid of negative influences in their lives. The really hard work comes in opening up to someone else again. Can they trust intimacy and closeness again? Do they even know to do that in a healthy way?

Boundaries keep some things out, but they also let some things in. Thus, boundary work goes in both directions, working to make sure that we keep a *balance* between vulnerability and safety, between open and closed, between self and other. Crucially, this comes from knowing ourselves, and learning that we are always in control of where that boundary is drawn.

It's not that any particular boundary is good or bad, rather that our own ability to manage ourselves and the demands of the world is developed to a greater or lesser extent.

We can have boundaries that might generally be considered harsh, but the manner in which we communicate these boundaries can make a massive difference. Say you don't like hugs. You can respond to a violation of this boundary by either lashing out at the offender, or politely declining any approaches for hugs and expressing your discomfort.

While you need not go into detail about the reasons behind your discomfort, other situations might demand some vulnerability on your part. Not only do both reactions project different versions of you, but they also reinforce certain types of behavior that may or may not be desirable. A good boundary is one that works for you and your life. It's a line that allows you to engage intimately with others while still maintaining a sense of healthy separateness. It's something you feel in control of, and which fits your values, needs, and desires. It may be that the woman in our example eventually does decide that she'd like to draw a boundary around sexuality entirely. She may take the path of celibacy or prioritize something else entirely. Culture, family, and the expectations of others are always present, but that doesn't mean we are not still in charge of choosing the boundaries that work best for us.

We can be said to lack boundaries any time we feel someone else's needs, desires, or power pushing into our world and dominating over our own wishes for our body, mind, and soul. When we feel like we have substituted someone else's story, needs, or information for our own, we can be sure that a boundary has been intruded upon. On the other hand, an absence of much-wanted intimacy or regular conflict and misunderstanding are signs that your boundaries are too rigid and inflexible. Childhood experiences and relationships with others can all affect where we place our boundaries, causing us to be too open to the world and the whims of others, or else shutting off entirely and building a wall around ourselves.

Finding the Balance

Bearing in mind that the only one who gets to decide on good or bad is you, take a look at how the following boundaries can be tweaked to make them more or less rigid.

Sexual or physical boundaries

Too porous: Not asking a partner to wear a condom despite wanting them to (underlying belief: I am not worth protecting, and my desires and needs are not important).

Too rigid: I don't trust other people at all and have sworn off dating to avoid being close to them (underlying belief: I cannot tolerate uncertainty or risk being hurt; all people are bad; the world is fundamentally hostile and unsafe).

Balanced boundary: I don't feel threatened or offended if my partner asks me to do something they like in bed, but I also feel comfortable saying "no" if I'm not interested (underlying belief: sex is safe and it's OK for different people to want different things, and express those wants. Someone having a want doesn't force me to fulfill it).

Emotional boundaries

Too porous: Regularly answering late-night calls from a friend who seems to constantly be in crisis, despite it interfering with your sleep and well-being (underlying belief: it's my job to rescue people from their own negative emotions, and I have no other value than this).

Too rigid: Refusing to show *any* concern or support to a friend in need (underlying belief: people are on their own in this world, and it's dangerous to get overwhelmed by other people's drama).

Balanced boundary: You never answer the phone after a certain hour at night. In the morning, you send your friend a supportive message and offer to chat for short periods, or offer helpful suggestions if they seem to have the same problem over and over again (underlying belief: you can help people without completely sacrificing yourself to them, or becoming their sole savior).

Mental, intellectual, spiritual or time boundaries

Too porous: You allow family members to constantly put you down over your beliefs or ideas (underlying belief: I have to fit in to be loved; everyone has to be the same; they are right and I'm wrong).

Too rigid: You refuse to budge on your position, and insist on doing things your way despite belonging to a family unit (underlying belief: I have to always maintain control; other people can't be trusted to do things properly).

Balanced boundary: You understand that you and your partner have big differences in your beliefs, but you respect one another and have both made the occasional compromise because you love one another (underlying belief: difference is not a threat; you can compromise sometimes because you value harmony and cohesion over being "right").

As you can see, a truly healthy boundary is about you and your needs. But in the context of other people and *their* needs, it's that sweet spot in between your identity and the world at large, where you can find happiness and well-being while still having enough flex in your boundaries to allow the good stuff in: joy, intimacy, closeness, and trust.

Having said that, it isn't enough to just have boundaries—we must know the right way to enforce them, as well. Going back to the example with the women in chapter one, both of them are aware of their boundaries. The problem mainly lies in knowing the right way to establish them. If you have a certain boundary, you need not enforce it unfailingly. Say you're not uncomfortable with anyone calling you past 10pm.

You can make exceptions to this rule depending on your preferences, like if there is an emergency that could use your involvement. Having good boundaries means both coming up with healthy limits and knowing the appropriate ways of enforcing them in different situations.

With good boundaries...
- You love others, but you also love yourself.

- You can say "no"... *and* hear it from others, knowing that everyone has the right to assert a limit.

- You know that you never need to compromise on your safety, values, well-being, etc., and you also respect that you should not cajole, convince, or beg someone else to behave as you want them to.

- You refuse to allow others to use your time, your emotions, your skills, your body, or anything else without your permission—and you also understand that you are not entitled to any of that from anyone else.

- You do not allow others to make you responsible for their emotions, and you refrain from blaming others, playing victim, or waiting for someone to take care of you.

- You see your emotions, ideas, thoughts, and fears as on par with everyone else's—you have as much right to speak up and act as anyone else does.

- You want relationships based on mutual caring and love; you do not want to fix anyone else, and you know that the only one who can fix you is you.

- You make compromises when you want to, never because you feel forced, dominated, or pressured. You value intimacy and can choose closeness—but you know that you are allowed to pull back if you want to.

- You are helpful, compassionate, and caring to others—but you always weigh your own well-being with others' and never "set yourself on fire to keep others warm"!

It would be too easy to simply have a list of "good" and "bad" boundaries—but the irony is that it's typically people with poor boundaries who seek assurance and excessive guidance from others, asking them to *tell* them how to live their lives. There is no rule book. As you know by now, boundary setting is our responsibility alone, and nobody can tell us what we are most comfortable with.

Even if you come across boundaries that seem like ones you want to adopt for yourself, it is important that you do so out of your own volition, and not because it was suggested to you. This will help you cultivate a sense of freedom and autonomy as you live by rules that you have chosen yourself. As children, we outsource different essential components of our lives as a matter of necessity. Yet, these habits often persist well into adulthood, making it customary for us to rely on others to think and decide for us.

Shedding this habit of dependence is key to living a life with healthy boundaries. As you work on your boundaries, ask yourself the following:

Does this boundary actually serve *me* (my wants, needs, limits, and overall values)?

What are my needs, and is this boundary helping me to meet them?

Is this boundary actually appropriate?

How does my boundary interact with the rights of others?

How does my boundary interact with my culture and context?

What effect do my boundaries have on me, and do I want this?

How could my boundary be improved?

Between a Rock and a Hard Place: Emotional Drain and Loneliness

The cells in every tissue and organ of your body have boundaries, too—semi-permeable membranes that selectively allow in certain substances while remaining closed off to others. It's a way of being *conditionally* open, so as to maintain a balanced equilibrium internally.

Psychologically, people aren't much different. If too much is coming in (other people's needs, criticisms, control, etc.) you are likely to feel overwhelmed, supersensitive, stressed out, anxious, flooded with negative emotions, on edge, or even a little numb. Everything is too much—you may find yourself overeating to fill the void, self-medicating, overworking, overextending yourself, or feeling like life is one drama after another, with people's emotions so close they almost feel like they could be your own.

While a porous membrane between you and the big wide world puts you in closer contact with everyone and everything else, it also shuts you out—from yourself. Being disconnected from your own needs, you may even subconsciously hope that letting others walk all over you will somehow redeem you, give you value, or inspire others to take care of you. Weak boundaries, whatever they are, result in an energy imbalance.

People with poorly defined boundaries may constantly feel exhausted. Why wouldn't you? If your energy is constantly being used to further someone else's agenda, while your own goals go ignored, how could you feel anything other than depleted and run-down?

Overly rigid boundaries signal an energy imbalance, as well. A cell in the body may be too open to water and absorb it indiscriminately, leading it to swell and swell, eventually bursting. But a membrane that never allows any water to enter will suffer the opposite problem: it will slowly start to shrivel and shrink. The psychological equivalent is loneliness.

Some people shut out what is hurtful and harmful, but go too far and shut out the good *and* the bad. By closing themselves off to everything, they lose out on intimacy, closeness to others, a sense of community, a feeling of belonging, and being appreciated, witnessed, and valued by the group.

Loneliness, isolation, and deep feelings of alienation can all arise from boundaries that lack flexibility. This is the person who errs on the side of saying "no," never takes risks, never allows themselves to trust others, and defaults to the position of thinking that *everything* in life is a potential threat, rather than practicing discernment according to their needs. Black-and-white thinking leaves no room for compromise, for patience, for tolerance, or for a resilient attitude—or even for fun and a sense of humor! We simply say, "I can't cope with that," and turn away from it—even if the thing we are turning away from is what we want deep down.

Those with healthy boundaries understand that there is always an implicit cost to intimacy—it's the risk of being vulnerable. In loving, we always open ourselves up to losing that love. In showing ourselves to others, we risk them rejecting us. Nevertheless, human beings are not islands—a mature person understands that sooner or later, the potential pain of being social with other flawed human beings is worth the almost infinite benefits.

Overly rigid boundaries come with enormous anxiety and responsibility—a deep distrust and suspicion in the world and in others. These are the people who shoulder everything themselves, never asking for help, bravely marching on alone. Sometimes, we think of empowered people as pure individualists who need no one and who build their own way in life with zero help. But this is not a superpower. This is actually the picture of a person who is afraid of intimacy, and who is weaker because of this fear.

An empowered person is someone who knows how and when to ask for help, how and when to show vulnerability, and how and when to take a rest and let others care for them. While those with overly porous boundaries can get overwhelmed in others, losing any idea of themselves and their own needs, the person with overly rigid boundaries can feel like their small self is all they have in this big, anonymous world—a self that is unconnected, unloved, irrelevant to anything or anyone else. You never open up to others and they never open up to you. You live in world of strangers, like an alien amongst humans, with nobody to share yourself with.

Between these two unhappy extremes is where the healthy person lives. Their boundaries are those in the perfect Goldilocks zone—firm enough to keep you feeling comfortable, respected, and safe from all of those things that could potentially drain or harm you, and yet flexible and permeable enough to allow in love and intimacy from those people who you want to be close to. And here lies the real magic of good boundaries: the thing that keeps out the bad, but lets in the good, *is the same thing*.

This bears some careful thinking. One strategy is to open up all the way and let everything in (including the bad); the other is to close all the way and leave everything out (including the good). The longer a person has practiced one or the other, the harder will it be to snap out of it and learn to live in the mean. Old habits die hard, but the effort will be worth the fulfilling life that comes with healthy boundaries.

The lesson here is that to become boundary masters, we *need* to learn to work in the grey areas, in the wiggle room in between extremes, and in those nuanced spaces. We also need to understand some core truths about what it means to be human: that we are *both* individuals and social beings. That we are all alone and sufficient unto ourselves, *and* we are also desperately and forever interconnected with one another. That sometimes, being close and intimate is scary, and sometimes being a proud individual is lonely and pointless—and that we can navigate all of these things if we know ourselves and constantly commit to serving our own needs as we serve others.

It's at the boundary between self and other that all of the interesting life stuff happens. If you have boundary issues, understand that you don't merely have a psychological quirk that needs fixing—rather, you are doing important work in one of the most fundamental areas of the human experience. Remember to have compassion for yourself, as well as for others, as you figure it all out!

A Simple Pyramid

This is another way to think about the fact that not all boundaries are created equal. The violation of some boundaries might leave you deeply hurt, while others are often only mild annoyances. As such, it is helpful to divide your boundaries into three categories depending on the level of importance you attach to them. This will help you navigate the most appropriate way to react when your boundaries are violated. These three categories are: essential boundaries, desired boundaries, and 'cherry-on-top' boundaries.

Starting backwards, cherry-on-top boundaries are those that aren't necessary for your well-being, but ones you'd love to have anyway. Consider this example. Say you're someone who doesn't watch television, but your mother is the kind of person who keeps her TV on throughout the day. When you decide to visit her for a couple of days, the droning noise from the television becomes a constant inconvenience. However, it might be inappropriate to ask her to turn it off since you're in her house.

In such cases, you can ask for the TV to be turned off at particular times to establish a boundary. Another example may be that you want your spouse to inform you whenever they're going to be late from work. Neither of these examples are deal-breakers for your relationships, yet they are boundaries which, when set effectively, can help you accomplish small things you desire. Don't fret if these feel like a reach or being too demanding; what matters is the way you communicate and handle them.

Next are desired boundaries. Though all three types of boundaries are ones that you desire in some way, desired boundaries are the ones that fall in between those that are essential and those that you can do without, but prefer to have. Let's consider another example. One of your friends constantly messages you during the day when you're at work and expects prompt replies. You can't afford to forego your work to chat with a friend, and the messaging is making you feel some resentment towards them. In such cases, you can ask them to not message you during your working hours unless the matter is urgent. What makes this a desired boundary is that this kind of behavior might be tolerable as long as your friend doesn't pressure you to reply frequently, but it is important enough for your well-being that you're compelled to express it.

Lastly, we have essential boundaries. These are the ones you absolutely need to enforce and whose violations you are not willing to tolerate any further. To reuse the previous example, your friend may be getting upset at you for not replying quickly. You believe that this expectation is unreasonable and are not willing to entertain it any longer. Another example may be this. Your friend repeatedly asks you intrusive questions about your personal life that you are uncomfortable answering. Despite repeated attempts, you can't seem to discourage them from asking. You might decide that such questions are no longer acceptable, and are willing to take the necessary steps towards protecting yourself.

This pyramid of boundaries is a great way to create an inventory of the boundaries you are attempting to establish. Which boundary falls into which category is completely up to you, and you need not worry about how others might categorize them. Write them down, and create different pyramids for different people if needed. Having your boundaries listed out will be invaluable when the time comes to establish them.

It Takes Two to Tango

Healthy boundaries are, in truth, more of a result and effect of good self-esteem than they are a cause of it. Similarly, a great relationship typically demonstrates great boundaries because it is a great relationship, and simply fixing boundary issues in a poor relationship may not be enough to magically turn it into a good one. Good boundaries make healthy people, and healthy people make good boundaries!

Whether you are single, partnered, breaking up, or recovering from a breakup, it always pays to figure out *how you can be the kind of person who naturally has excellent boundaries.* If you are starting from a place of low self-esteem, practicing healthy boundaries can slowly grow your sense of worth in your own identity, and it's this sense that will, in turn, make it easier for you to keep on with good boundaries—it's a "virtuous cycle."

On the other hand, those who generally have healthy boundaries might find themselves undermining themselves with their partners due to our tendency to treat romantic relationships differently from other types of bonds. As such, even if you naturally have excellent boundaries, you may nevertheless struggle to enforce or maintain them in relationships.

Many people first become aware of boundary issues in the context of romantic relationships. All of the warning signs are the same, but in this playing field, you may detect the presence of poor boundaries by:

- Black-and-white thinking: either you are absolutely awful or an innocent angel (nothing in between!) and your partner is similarly all or nothing.
- Finding yourself way too invested and attached to a person after only knowing them a short while.
- Often finding yourself feeling defensive, guilty, caught up in weird arguments you can't seem to get out of, blaming one another, or feeling "crazy."

- Taking responsibility for your partner's actions ("he didn't mean to, he just has a bad temper…") or else being unable to take responsibility for yourself and your actions.
- Relationships where "opposites attract"—you are either dramatically and hopelessly in love with someone who is not that available, or feel distant and unable to commit yourself—or you both could switch roles as the "pursuer" and the "pursued." For example, a person willing to take the blame for everything may find themselves with a person who is happy to blame everyone else for their problems.
- Feeling controlled by your partner or wanting to control them; experiencing issues of jealousy.
- One or both of you feel like you *need* rather than *want* the other one, and there are patterns of dependency, even blackmail and coercion.

- Your relationship feels like a roller coaster—you never feel quiet, secure, and calm about where you stand.
- There's game playing and manipulation.
- You feel like you can't ever let go of your partner, and that you're incomplete without them—they alone can ensure your happiness.
- You feel like you sacrifice a lot for the relationship and that you compromise many of your needs in order to earn love (usually, you don't get much out of the deal!).

In classic codependent relationships, the dynamic is one built on faulty boundaries—one person unconsciously agrees to be overly responsible for the other's happiness, while the other unconsciously agrees to not be responsible for their emotions or actions. This is the familiar pattern between narcissists and empaths, saviors and their misunderstood "rescue projects," abusers and their victims, emotionally avoidant people and their needy partners, hell-bent on spending their lives chasing, rescuing, and fixing someone who refuses to be chased, rescued, or fixed.

In codependent relationships, a victim creates problems because they unconsciously feel like this will make others love them. The rescuer leaps in to help, because they unconsciously believe that saving and serving others will give them value and make others love them. Though the needs on both sides are genuine, the method of satisfying these needs is doomed to fail. The relationship becomes a vicious cycle where both partners feel as though they're *temporarily* getting what they need, but ultimately, their behavior wears away their self-esteem and healthy sense of identity. The behavior goes on and on, satisfying nobody.

The "victims" in these dynamics (i.e., the one with too porous boundaries) can only heal when they strengthen their own identity enough to understand what they want and need. Through this, they can set boundaries and take responsibility for their own happiness. They have to release the belief that others are responsible for their unhappiness, or that they will achieve wellness and wholeness by rescuing others. Such "victims" (they are not really victims at all) need to shift their focus away from other people's needs and onto their own, knowing deep down that they have value without needing to take on the blame, responsibility, or rescue role for others.

When a person with weak boundaries can do this, they will no longer attract or maintain relationships with people who have boundary issues that are complementary to their own. Rather, they will attract people on the basis of their mature, conscious, healthy self-esteem. It's not uncommon for a person to develop healthier boundaries and self-identity and find that their relationship ends—this is not a failure, but a sign that this person has grown and evolved. If they can seek out a new partner who respects and holds them accountable to their own boundaries, they can grow a healthier relationship from day one.

It may be easier to build a healthy relationship from the inside out and do the work necessary to cultivate confidence and self-worth first, regardless of what others do or don't do. This way, we make our own psychological growth our first responsibility, and we don't wait for someone else to help us or blame a poor relationship for our never making a change.

Good Boundary Mantras:

- I am not responsible for the emotions of others. It is not my job to live others' lives, only to live my own.
- I will not let guilt, shame, or fear drive my actions. I will not blame others for my choices, nor accept blame from others for their choices.
- I will not try to control others, nor will I accept someone trying to control me.
- I deserve love and respect as I am, right now. I do not need to rescue or fix others, I do not need to play helpless, and I do not need to manipulate others to be worthy of love and respect.

- I do things because I want to, not because I have to. I know what I want because I know who I am.
- It is my job to know, communicate, and assert my needs. I always have the right and responsibility to walk away from those who violate my boundaries.

Takeaways

- It is all too easy to fall into the trap of replacing loose boundaries with ones that are overly rigid. We might feel like we are protecting ourselves by erecting a huge emotional wall around us, but in truth, we are simply insulating ourselves from positive experiences that are necessary to live a fulfilling life. As such, we must discover the mean that lies between these two types of boundaries. Those are the ones that we should aim to integrate into our daily lives.
- Boundaries that are too weak will inevitably be an emotional drain on

our mental health. When we keep such boundaries, we implicitly allow others to trample over us. This leads to us feeling used, unappreciated, and taken for granted. On the other hand, rigid boundaries can make us feel extremely lonely. It is understandable to be defensive and overprotective if we have been betrayed or hurt by those closest to us, but keeping everyone at an arm's length only leaves us feeling alone and uncared for.

- The key to setting good boundaries is to focus on what feels comfortable to *you*, and nobody else. It can be tempting to look up and simply copy the kind of boundaries we think we *should* have, but ultimately, if we want to live a free life, we have to live by our own rules. This doesn't mean that we never compromise or be flexible. Negotiating interactions always involves some give-and-take. The important thing here is that the giving and taking are something that

we both consent to and are willing to accept.
- All great romantic relationships are based on healthy boundaries set up by both parties. Even if you're starting from a place of low self-worth, with some perseverance, you, too, can be the type of person who naturally has healthy boundaries in relationships.

Chapter Four: Knowing Thyself

How do you have good relationships?

Part of it is having good boundaries.

How do you have good boundaries?

You take responsibility for asserting your needs, wants, and limits.

How do you know what your needs, wants, and limits are?

You know *yourself*.

A boundary issue is ultimately about identity.

It's about understanding who you are as a person, and all of the shapes and contours that make up your personality, your values, your unique set of likes and dislikes. But if you have boundary issues, this may not seem like an easy thing to figure out. You may have put others' needs ahead of your own for so long that you don't even *know* what you want or don't want. You may need to take some time to firm up your preferences or, in some cases, you may be finding all of this out for the very first time!

Your feelings are a clue. Your heart and body can alert you to your values and inner boundaries, even if you're not consciously and mentally aware of them yet. Remember that nobody else can tell you what *you* are comfortable with—only you know that. First of all, understand that you, as a human being, have human rights that are never allowed to be violated.

Even if you have low self-esteem, you can rest assured that you have the right to say "no" without guilt, the right to respect, the right to have needs, and the right to make a mistake and learn from it. For some people, it can be incredibly healing to simply acknowledge that they have a right to have boundaries in the first place. They need to constantly remind themselves: *I matter. What I want and don't want matters.*

Next, check in with your gut. It's true that a lifetime of poor parenting, bad relationships, and faulty cultural programing can result in people who feel very weakly connected to their own boundaries. But if you become quiet and check in with your body, you can still hear the voice of your intuition. Notice how your shoulders tighten when your boss enters the room. Becomes curious about that heavy feeling at the back of your throat when your partner insults you. Examine that awful sensation in the pit of your stomach when a family member is shaming you for something. These are all your body's way of saying, "That went too far. That crossed a boundary."

Ask yourself (often!) who you are and what you stand for. Your identity informs your values, and your values inform your boundaries. If you know that you are a kind and compassionate person, then you automatically know that one of your values is to protect and care for animals. This, in turn, tells you that one of your boundaries is, "I will not tolerate anyone hurting my pets, and I will never hurt an animal myself." Now, if a family member or friend kicks your dog one day, you can act immediately and decisively. You put down a boundary and mean it: "Nobody hurts my dog. If you do that again, you are no longer welcome in my house."

Without a clear idea of your identity, it's harder to settle on firm values and you're likely to set boundaries that are not as relevant, or are maybe just the expectations and pressures you've absorbed from others! As you work on your boundaries, take the time to convert your value statements into boundaries that can be practically asserted.

How much do you really want to sacrifice—i.e., how much time, energy and other resources do you have? What makes you uncomfortable? What matters most to you and what are absolutely not your priorities in life? Are you placing enough energy and attention on your priorities? Is your focus primarily on your own needs or on others'? Boundaries are not black and white—what is nonnegotiable for you and what can you be a little more flexible on? What things are you happy to compromise over?

Too many people wait until their boundaries have been crossed to start looking at these boundaries and improving them. But most of the good work of boundaries happens long *before* you encounter another person and their behavior. For example, someone may know that they have boundary issues at work.

Historically, this has always been the case for them, so when they start a new job, they take the time to outline a proactive strategy. They look carefully at their values, priorities, and available time and energy, and decide on a hard limit of work hours beyond which they are not comfortable committing to. Knowing this in advance, they are prepared the next time they are pushed to work overtime on a public holiday.

They use carefully phrased "I" statements to politely, but assertively, state their boundary, and then follow through. In this way, the person affirms their right to their own preferences and communicates to others that their time and well-being are important. Such a person may find with time that it becomes easier to be assertive this way.

Oftentimes, you will also be faced with unforeseen situations where you need to think on your feet and decide whether something violates your boundaries. Say you're out with your friends and one of them suggests doing something that you're uncomfortable with, but the others aren't. It could be a prank, drugs, or something else.

You might think to yourself that some flexibility in your boundaries might be warranted. Yet, you might just be falling prey to peer pressure in the moment. In such instances, it is imperative that you respect your needs and comfort above appearing cool and easy-going. If the thought of doing something makes you uncomfortable, actually doing it will likely not make you feel any better. The more difficult a particular boundary area is for you, the more detailed your planning and strategy may have to be.

You may decide, in dating, that you are simply not comfortable having dates that sprawl on longer than an hour because you find them draining. You may decide that you won't answer online dating messages or texts during work hours or when you're with your family. You may decide that no matter what anyone says, you are not comfortable dating outside of a particular age range, for example. Your boundaries may be more abstract—if a date flops or someone turns out to be rude, you make a promise to yourself to not allow that negative energy to seep into the rest of your life.

You draw a boundary and tell yourself, "No matter what happens, I'm not going to get cynical, or respond with rudeness myself. I won't give up, but I also won't allow any dating disappointments to bring down my mood."

Start with who you are. Know yourself and know what you want and don't want. Then, allow yourself to set a boundary. Ask what you're trying to achieve with this boundary—is it to protect yourself? Is it to maintain more life balance or communicate more self-worth to others? Once you've set your goal, think about realistic and practical ways to assert and defend your boundary if necessary. And though it seldom comes to it, you need to consider what you will do if people *don't* respect your boundaries.

"I" Statements

Boundaries involve other people, but they are primarily about you. When you formulate boundaries, keep yourself and your needs in the center.

We've seen that it can be tricky to assert your own needs without trampling on the rights of others. This is especially hard for people who initially over-accommodate and then reach their breaking point all at once and lash out, long past the point at which their boundary was crossed.

Phrase boundaries in terms of *your* feelings, values, needs, and limits, and not what the other person does or doesn't do. This will help you get a sense of control and responsibility over your own emotional well-being, all the while never implying that others are responsible for it. Along with this, you can either suggest an arrangement that you feel will be more suitable for both of you, or specify what you would like the other person to do to help ameliorate the situation.

"When you ask me to do the washing up when it's your turn to do it, I feel anxious and taken advantage of, because it feels like I am not valued. I feel happier when you complete your share of the chores when you say you will."

"When I work on weekends, I feel run-down and resentful, because my family is more important than my job. I need to be able to have my weekends free of work obligations."

"When others make comments about what I'm wearing, I feel attacked and judged. What I need is for people to give me respect to be as I am without commenting on it."

If someone asks you to do their chores for them, asks you to work on the weekend, or makes a snide remark about your clothing, you can simply say "no" or remove yourself from the conversation. If you've spent the time understanding and communicating your needs, your values, etc., you may be surprised to find that people seldom press the issues, anyway.

They will naturally sense what your limits are and believe you! If you can politely and calmly say "no" to someone gently pressing your boundary, you will only strengthen their esteem of you (and a person who doesn't respect it has immediately shown you that they are not a person you need to be around).

However, there are some instances where "I" statements may not work. They can often be perceived as veiled accusations, which only ends up inviting a defensive response that ultimately does not solve the underlying issue. Take the first example mentioned above.

The person being asked to complete their share of the chores might easily choose to focus on only the first half of the statement, "I feel anxious and taken advantage of." That person could feel that you're saying that they intended to take advantage of you or make you feel anxious. In such cases, it might be helpful to be slightly vulnerable in the emotions you choose to express and the way you form the "I" statement. Say you're annoyed by your spouse repeatedly coming home late and not eating dinner with you.

Instead of saying that you feel disrespected or unappreciated, expressing the fact that you felt lonely or unwanted might help you deliver your message in a more constructive manner.

You in Relation to Others

Once you know who *you* are, you can begin to see yourself more clearly in relation to others. It begins to seem more and more obvious to you what is right and what is wrong, comfortable and uncomfortable, healthy and unhealthy. An unintended side effect, unfortunately, of developing better boundaries and self-worth is that it will immediately show you who complements you regarding anything *other* than these terms. By saying "no," you may reveal all of those people who always expected a "yes."

Sometimes, it can be quite shocking to see how others respond to your growing sense of confidence and self-compassion. You may be surprised to see just how invested others were in having you be just exactly what they wanted, regardless of your needs or well-being—and you may see some poor behavior designed to guilt, frighten, or shame you back into poor boundaries again. Whenever we grow, there will be some areas of our lives that no longer fit us anymore. Those who care about you as a person will welcome and celebrate your healthier boundaries; those who merely enjoyed what you could do for them will not be pleased, and will call you selfish and mean.

What is the state of your relationships right now? Not only can examining our relationships with others be valuable in itself, it's also an exercise that can mirror back to us our own problematic boundaries. Whether it's a colleague or boss, romantic partner, family member, or friend, and whether it's current or a relationship from the past, our involvement with others can show us loudly and clearly what we think of ourselves.

What were your boundaries like with your parents, the people who were your first caregivers and role models for all subsequent human relationships? Were they too rigid? Too loose? Many people can look into the past and see the roots of poor boundaries with parents that were too demanding, too intrusive, too enmeshed. Can you see any echoes from your earliest relationships today? If you're having trouble identifying anything concrete, you might phrase the question differently: What lessons did you learn as you grew up about who you were, what you were here for, what your value was, and what your rights and responsibilities were? Every family has its unspoken "rules" about love, worth, and belonging—what were yours?

As you move closer to the present, look at the key people in your life and the quality of your connection with them. You can probably think of some people who deliberately stepped on your boundaries, but are there any more general patterns you can spot? Self-help literature abounds with descriptions of "toxic people," but the truth is that no person is an island, sitting alone, toxic all by themselves.

Rather, what *is* toxic is a relationship, a dynamic, a story that two or more people agree to tell *together*. Have you played a role in any toxic stories? Maybe you were always the victim, or the rescuer, or the people-pleaser, or the wallflower who never spoke up. Or, maybe, you were the person who was "hurt too many times" and withdrew completely, building a high wall and daring anybody to care enough to try and climb it.

Though our discussions on these topics tend to describe such traits and situations as straightforward or easily discernible, we as humans are great at being insidiously toxic without realizing it. A mother who steps on her child's boundaries purely out of love and care is still being toxic due to her unwillingness to respect her child's desires above her own. As such, identifying harmful patterns and toxicity will invariably require serious thought and reflection into the nature of our relationships. If we discover that we were the ones being toxic, we must be humble enough to be able to admit it and try to improve to the best of our capabilities.

What about your romantic relationship right now (if you have one)? It can be hardest of all to spot unhealthy boundaries here because much of what we're taught as a culture is normal is really not normal. People in love songs sing about not being able to live without the other one, Valentine's day cards claim, "You complete me," and we think that the couple who does everything together is cute. We tell young girls that jealousy proves a man's love for you, or watch rom-coms where the male lead is basically a stalker.

Poor boundaries in a relationship don't always look like abuse and drama. Some of the less obvious signs include a partner constantly "checking up" on you, getting angry that you don't text or call often enough, being nosy, verifying where you are and asking precisely when you'll get back… the unconscious message seems to be: "You need to be available for me and my needs, always." It's a boundary violation on one's time and it's controlling. However, when in love, we can easily mistake these for signs of love and strong attachment due to our faulty impressions of what it means to be a good partner.

If one of both of you cannot seem to make a decision without the other, it suggests enmeshment and a sense of identity too wound up in the relationship. You need to be able to confidently know what you want, independent and irrespective of what the other wants. Similarly, a partner who is "protective" may seem great, but it can go too far—you should never feel infantilized, dependent, or helpless. This can also be a ploy to control, i.e., "I'm just doing what's best for you," or, "I only crossed that boundary because I'm trying to help you."

It's an enormous red flag if they invade your privacy (go through your phone, your personal belongings, your journal, etc.). If one or both of you is insecure and needs constant validation and reassurance, this is also a sign of boundary issues and can quickly set one of you up as the nurturer or rescuer. Watch out for drama and a sense of all or nothing, high-stakes thinking. Everyone misses their partner when they're gone, but your world shouldn't fall to pieces if your partner goes away for a few days!

Finally, watch out for a partner who forgets about everything else in their life except for you, or encourages you to do the same, for example, demanding you stop seeing friends and family. These are all red flags that a relationship dynamic is unhealthy.

Recognizing Abuse

But what if you're dealing with an outright abusive person who refuses to respect your boundaries? The above red flags can be unintentional and a result of a partner themselves having issues establishing healthy boundaries. These can be helped with compassionate awareness, counseling, and reevaluating the relationship.

Truly "toxic" dynamics, however, take things a bit further. That is the realm of deliberate, outright abuse when a person knowingly oversteps a boundary and does so for their own benefit. A relationship with such a person can be very dangerous, especially if the person whose boundaries are being obliterated doesn't even understand what is happening. They may stay trapped in the dysfunction because they believe they deserve it, they believe it's good for them, they feel sorry for their abuser, or worse—they simply believe that this is what love looks like. In such a relationship, counseling and frank conversation will seldom be enough.

Those with a poor sense of identity and low self-worth can quickly become engulfed in unhealthy dynamics, unable to see that their boundaries are slowly being worn away and their well-being damaged. A boundary is like the soul's immune system—without an immune system, the body would quickly become overrun with infection, and it's no different with our emotional or spiritual body. Some people are so embroiled in drama, demands, coercion, threats, guilt, shame, fear, and manipulation that it becomes invisible to them. They simply think, "This is what love feels like," or, "This is just how a marriage goes."

If you have especially weak boundaries, it's quite possible that you have attracted or are currently attracting the kind of person who lives to play with, exploit, or push the boundaries of others for their own ends. It will help immensely to understand *how* your boundaries are being violated. As always, trust your gut and tune into your own body and soul to check if certain situations, people, or behaviors truly align with how you see yourself and what you want from the world. A toxic relationship can mirror back unconscious beliefs of self-hatred within you—people in the external world who treat you like you are worthless may only be confirming your own *internal* belief in exactly the same thing.

Watch out for "psychological urgency" in relationships. This is the feeling that if your partner calls, you had better quickly jump into action for them, or else. If you feel rushed or as though you have to act a certain way before time, resources, or patience wears out, you're being manipulated.

The person who suddenly texts, "Get dressed and be ready in 20 minutes, I'm taking us out to dinner," is not really being romantic; they're forcing you to quickly make an impulsive decision without thinking and just do what they want. There should always be room for you to think and respond—be careful if you always feel hurried along.

In the beginning of a relationship, watch out for other intensely "romantic" gestures that are designed to overwhelm and disorient you. Watch out for game-playing or people trying to "win" or capture you. Sending flowers to your house every day, begging for a date, turning up unannounced with gifts, consulting friends and family about your schedule so they know where you are and can "surprise" you.

Initially, you might be in awe of the time and attention someone else is devoting towards impressing you, but these actions may or may not be well-intentioned. The effect is the same regardless: you are disempowered and put on the back foot because saying "no" will invariably be perceived as rude and thankless. Not to mention, what happens if you turn down these advances? Sadly, too many women know how quickly a man can go from declaring that she's a goddess among women to wishing her dead—all because she said "no."

In the early stages of a relationship, try not to see what the other person is doing to earn a "yes" and rather how ready they are to accept your "no."

Once a relationship is underway, abuse is often characterized by a general lack of concern for your emotional well-being. If you constantly feel confused, on edge, and uneasy, it's not a "passionate relationship"—it's a problem. Stonewalling (shutting you out, ignoring you, or refusing to talk to you as punishment) or gaslighting (trying to make you appear crazy and irrational or doubt your own judgment) are hallmarks of abusers and narcissists hell-bent on controlling others.

It goes without saying that a lack of concern for your physical health and safety is also a giant red flag and violates your fundamental human rights. You should never be forced to do things that frighten you or put you in danger.

Abusers will knowingly chip away at your privacy, your time, and your self-esteem. They will feel *entitled to you as a resource*—they will believe that they deserve to have parts of you: your time, your sexuality, your kindness, your attention. They will enjoy what you provide for them, but this is completely different from appreciating you as a person and valuing you. Ask yourself, does your partner love you or do they love what they can get from you?

All kinds of manipulation can get you in the position they want you in—they may grind you down slowly, use fear to control you, put you down so that you don't feel entitled to say "no" or feel how you feel, call you crazy, "test" you, make you walk on eggshells, be unfair, refuse to communicate, be sneaky, blow hot and cold, punish you with silence or sulking, pick fights, rewrite history (especially if it makes them look bad), or use the classic "DARVO" response—Deny, Attack, and Reverse Victim and Offender."

For example, a woman may try to hold her partner accountable for hurting her arm in an argument, and he will respond with, "I *didn't* hurt you just now. How dare you suggest that I would ever lay a hand on you?! This is the problem right here—I'm just trying to talk to you, and you get so crazy about things. You're so dramatic and it's wearing me down."

The list of ways that abusers can abuse is endless, sadly. But it all amounts to the same thing—all of these tactics are mere tools in the inventory of a person who would like to push past your boundaries to get what they want. This is a person who consciously or unconsciously believes that others are not free agents in their own right, but merely resources to exploit, or means to an end.

They believe that their own desires and wants are more important than other people's rights or well-being. A person who loves and respects you will care about your wants and needs, and will never trample over them to satisfy themselves. Having a strong sense of identity, self-worth, and intact boundaries will alert you immediately to this parasitic and exploitative behavior. Your boundaries are protective barriers around what you love and value in yourself, and they say to potential abusers, "*That* is not what my heart, body, and mind are for. I am not a thing for anybody to use."

Your Role, Your Needs

This leads nicely to the obvious question: What *are* you for then, if not to fulfill the selfish needs of someone who doesn't care about you? You cannot answer this question without understanding your own identity, needs, rights, values, and desires. An enormous part of the problem in abusive or unhealthy relationships is the "victim's" hidden agreement to continue to allow themselves to be used in that way. Focused on the abuser's needs and wants, their own needs and wants are invisible, and they never have the chance to step up and experience themselves and their unique agency.

Enmeshed, damaged, or confused boundaries are those in which it is not at all clear what belongs to whom—a person feels as though they are to blame for the other's actions, another feels that their partner is responsible for making them happy, and nobody knows quite where one ends and the other begins. To start to unpick this mess, it's necessary to slow down and start looking carefully at the individuals in a dynamic.

What are everyone else's needs?

And what are your needs?

What is your partner entitled to?

And what are your rights?

People with poor boundaries will often forget to include themselves in the equation. They may spend their entire lives wondering why their partner does this or that, what their partner is thinking, what *they* want, what *they* mean, what *they* need, how to fix *them*, how to make *them* happy.

They become their partner's cheerleader, or therapist, or ATM, or parent, or police officer... it can start to feel like the relationship is just one person, with a less important helper who is merely there to facilitate! When you include your own needs and desires into the equation, however, you can start balancing things and moving your relationship towards a healthy, mature, and respectful equilibrium.

What happens after you assert your boundaries? This is important. Some people will respect and honor them. If you've identified, clarified, and communicated your boundaries loudly and clearly, you may feel better, but still find yourself faced with a person who simply does not agree with your new idea of being just as valuable as they are! Now what?

The scary truth is this: we cannot *make* a person respect our boundaries because we cannot make a person do anything. This is what many boundary-pushers don't ever understand: people are not meant to be controlled. We cannot make someone respect, or love, or value us. But we can always respect and love and value ourselves, and we can always choose what *we* do.

Sometimes, in relationships, a frustrated partner will issue a harsh ultimatum, but go back on it when the other half refuses to capitulate. The misunderstanding is that an ultimatum is a way to control what another person does. But it isn't—it's a way to clarify and state what *you* will do.

So, to answer the question of what to do when people violate your boundaries: it's up to you.

It's your decision to make, but the following questions can help you narrow down to the best course of action.

Question 1: Is there some wiggle room on this boundary, and could you compromise, sacrifice, or let it go?

Healthy relationships require some level of compromise. Nobody gets what they want 100% of the time, at least not in a world shared by others. Is the boundary that's been crossed a nonnegotiable one, or are you happy to bend it a little to accommodate the other person for the sake of the relationship?

Importantly, the question is, are you *happy* to compromise? Not, do you feel guilty and coerced into compromising? You might be willing to make an exception if the benefits are greater than the losses of letting it slide. But be careful—it has to be something you're truly willing to do. Being a martyr who unconsciously expects that relinquishing their own needs entitles them to extra care later down the line is simply another form of manipulation.

Question 2: Can you identify a pattern of behavior?

A person pressing at a boundary could be doing so innocently, and may immediately stop if you let them know the boundary is there and why it exists. Someone may even make the same mistake another time in error. But do you find yourself repeatedly setting the same boundary? It may be a sign that you haven't actually followed through.

It's uncomfortable to admit, but oftentimes when people frequently dismiss our boundaries, it's because we ourselves don't take them all that seriously. It might be helpful to write down any boundary violations and keep a record of them. This is to keep clear and focused, and also to identify patterns. If you constantly tell people that they aren't allowed to do XYZ but there are no real consequences for them doing XYZ, they will only continue to do XYZ. A one-off occurrence can be forgiven; a pattern more strongly suggests that you need to follow through and respect your own boundary before expecting others to.

Keep in mind that not all boundary violations deserve the same reaction. Some boundaries are essential to our well-being, while others are more flexible. Reacting too strongly to some violations might not be appropriate and can sour important relationships in your life. At the same time, be firm about boundaries that have been violated repeatedly in communicating them, as well as enforcing any remedial measures.

Question 3: Is this person actually capable of respecting your boundaries?

It doesn't matter how legitimate your boundaries are, how well you communicate them, or how many second chances you give. Some people simply do not want to respect you, and probably never will. This can be extremely hard to swallow, especially if you're a kind and loving person yourself. But it's a little like repeatedly trying to have a civilized conversation with a ravenous lion, hoping time after time that it will stop trying to eat you.

Unfortunately, you might discover that the people you value most fit into this category. However, someone's importance in your life does not make their bad behavior less or more justifiable. If a friend, partner, parent, or relative has consistently shown an unwillingness to respect your boundaries, it is time to distance yourself from them physically and emotionally.

Question 4: How would you feel if you were to limit contact with this person or situation?

If you're not willing to compromise, if there is a repeated pattern of disrespect, and if the person can't or won't change, then you can start thinking of ways to minimize your exposure. Choosing to remain in a denigrating situation is, in a way, an act of self-abuse. It's true that we can't always run away from harmful people (for example, if they're our bosses or our parents), but we *always* have the choice to moderate our interactions.

We can look for another job, move out, or manage our time and personal space in such a way as to minimize contact. It may be a long and somewhat uncomfortable process to untangle ourselves from dynamics that have taken years to set up, but it can be done, and it starts with you remembering that you have a right to say "no."

Limiting contact is something that people see as harsh and unjustifiable. This is especially true when it comes to family, who might criticize you for your decision. Alternatively, singling out that one friend in your group for violating your boundaries might result in you being pressured to patch up the friendship. Regardless of the incentive to work things out, not all relationships or friendships can be fixed, and a clean break could be the best option for your mental health. You don't have to explain your decision to anyone. Consciously removing yourself from a damaging situation is not a punishment, an act of revenge, or a way to manipulate the other person into treating you better. When you walk away or limit contact, make sure you're doing it for *you*, and really mean it, understanding exactly why you need to do it.

If you feel bogged down by guilt, try to frame cutting down contact as a positive gesture. You are not shutting down, closing off, or running away from others, but rather opening up to them, listening to yourself, and respecting yourself and your own needs. Many people will frame minimizing contact as a zero-sum thing—that if you are kind to yourself it means that you must necessarily be mean to someone else. This is a lie. It's not always easy to practice self-care and to show ourselves the love we deserve, but we can do it, even if others don't like it.

The important thing to remember as you ask yourself these questions is that you always, *always* have choices. Sometimes, there may not be many of them, and sometimes, we may not like the choices we have. But as adults who are responsible for our own well-being, we can choose. The truth is that enforcing boundaries is easy. It's not hard to know that we don't like being mistreated. Then, why is it so difficult to manage boundaries? This brings us to a final, perhaps most difficult question:

Question 5: In what ways are you enabling the violation of your boundaries?

You are never to blame for someone mistreating you. However, if most of us are honest, sometimes the biggest impediment to us leaving a consistently toxic situation is *not* the other person—it's us. We quietly agree to their assessment that our boundaries are really not worth respecting. By staying, we unconsciously communicate that we agree with their low assessment of our value.

Maybe we are afraid of causing offense, or we are afraid of losing the relationship, even if it is a terrible one. Maybe we are afraid that poor treatment is all that we deserve and all that we'll ever find. Maybe we can't stand the thought of conflict or of another person disliking us. This is where the distinction between blaming ourselves and being responsible for how others treat us becomes important. Ultimately, nobody can mistreat us without our implicit permission. While the lack of an objection does not imply consent, this is a somewhat convenient way to escape responsibility for our lives.

This does not mean that we should beat ourselves up and wallow in guilt, but it does demand that we hold ourselves accountable for what happens to us. Once we assume this responsibility, it empowers us to recognize our agency and exercise control over our relations with others.

Rather than allowing our fears to control our behavior, though, we need to bring them out into the open, examine them, and dismantle them. What are the underlying beliefs? "I'm not worth good treatment;" "People will only love me if I sacrifice myself entirely;" "It's impossible for me to be alone;" "My job is to please people all the time, or else I'm worthless," and so on. Do you really want these (frankly incorrect) assumptions to sit at your core, driving all of your decisions? Or, would you rather be your own friend and ally and act in your best interests, knowing that you are and have always been worth happiness and love?

The Boundary Habit

Checking in on the state of your own identity and self-esteem and the state of your relationships is not something that you do once and never again. Healthy boundaries arise naturally as a consequence of how we feel about ourselves. The work we've been speaking about in this book concerns boundaries, but at its core it's not about how others do or do not treat us. *It's about our attitudes to ourselves*; how much we love and respect ourselves; how much we are willing to care for ourselves, to give ourselves what we need, to protect ourselves from what is damaging, to honor our own voice when we hear it.

Difficult boundaries with others point to a deeper relationship problem: the one we have with ourselves. If you truly and deeply know in your bones that you are a human being with inviolable value and rights, you will conduct yourself in the world in a way that inspires others to mirror the same back to you.

When we work on boundary issues, we can work at different levels. We can look at the individual situations or people involved in everyday life and work to manage them on a superficial level. We can also sink deeper and ask ourselves with more focus what our boundaries are and how we can have better ones. But we can sink *even* deeper and work at the level of our own self-esteem. This is the work that we do when we release those harmful negative beliefs that tell us we are worthless and unlovable.

As you read through this book, you may have noticed invitations to tackle your own boundary issues at different levels. You could have a heartfelt discussion with an intrusive friend, or simply avoid her, or you could start a boundaries journal and work on literal phrasing to use when politely saying "no." You could start every morning with an affirmation or prayer to re-affirm your self-love and right to respect and dignity. You could wake up every morning and tell yourself, "What I want and who I am matters."

All of these approaches will work, and they will mutually support one another. The more you can practically assert your boundaries in the real world, the more confident you'll feel, and the easier it will become to set those boundaries. You can set up healthy feedback loops, welcoming into your life those people who agree to treat you with love and respect and gradually saying goodbye to those who don't. It's work that cannot be rushed or faked, and it often comes in fits and starts. It's work that no one else can do for you, but it may be the most important work that you ever do!

Takeaways

- Your identity and relationship with boundaries are inextricably linked. Those with poor boundaries often struggle with them because they have never truly reflected upon what it is that they want. On the other hand, rigid boundaries are a sign of fear and insecurity about the world and its potential for causing pain to us. Our identity forms the basis for our values, and our values are instrumental to our boundaries. Only by cultivating an awareness of what our values are can we start to build healthy boundaries.
- We live in a world where everyone has boundaries, strong or weak. As such, we must be mindful of not only our own boundaries, but also those of the ones around us. If someone has overly rigid boundaries, they might end up stepping over our own. Alternatively, if we have loose boundaries, we might be subjected to abuse from those who enjoy controlling us for their own benefit. Anyone who repeatedly violates our

boundaries despite being warned is likely being abusive, and must be dealt with appropriately.
- "I" statements are an invaluable tool when it comes to communicating your boundaries to others. These statements aim to convey how particular actions committed by others make us feel. If, say, we are annoyed by our spouse not doing their share of chores, we might tell them "I feel anxious and taken for granted when you...".
- Sometimes, simply communicating your boundaries to others will not persuade them to stop violating them. In such cases, it might help to ask ourselves some questions regarding this person. Is there any wiggle room with respect to your boundaries? Is there a pattern of any type of behavior that you can discern? Is this person even capable or willing to accept your boundaries? Are you allowing or enabling the violation of your boundaries in some way? Considering the answers to

questions like these can help you determine the appropriate course of action when it comes to boundary violations.

Chapter Five: Boundaries, Brick by Brick

The journey to better boundaries is a journey of empowerment. We've spent some time understanding what boundaries actually are (and aren't!), how to recognize when you have poorly functioning boundaries, and hopefully, you've decided that you are worth better boundaries. Though this may seem great, at some point, you have to actually head out into the world and show up in a real and concrete way, as a person fundamentally different from how you were before.

This takes courage, patience, and self-love. It also takes a good strategy! Planning will give you a sense of control, purpose, and direction. Knowing what you want and how you're going to get it can focus your mind and give you strength to follow through on your convictions, despite any pushback from others.

Remember that the inner work informs the outer work. Part of healing your boundaries is doing the work of strengthening your self-esteem, refining your identity, and narrowing in on the values that give your life a sense of purpose and meaning. More practically speaking, though, boundary work is about taking the time to draw clear, detailed, and precise lines around yourself with a firm intention. The best plan will be one that you devise for yourself and stick to because you are convinced of its value and necessity in life. But in the meantime, see if the following steps inspire you to act with more empowerment and personal agency.

Step One: Get clear within yourself

This will come as no surprise. You cannot expect anyone to be aware of, let alone respect, a boundary that you never communicate. People can't read minds. Do you use passive aggression to hint at your needs and limits without stating them clearly? Your first step is to speak out, loudly and clearly.

Have you ever noticed how a dog will obey and respect one person in the household and completely walk all over another? That person can yell "Stop, don't you dare chew that!" as much as they'd like, and the dog simply dismisses them. Another person can simply *look* at the dog and the dog will instantly obey. Why? Because the dog is responding not just to the words, but to the energy and intention behind them. The dog may correctly sense that the first person doesn't really mean what they say. The dog knows what many humans know—that the boundary is there in name only, but not in spirit; that there are no real consequences for crossing such a "boundary."

Your first step is, as we've been exploring in the previous chapters, to align well within yourself. There is no boundary without a strong, healthy sense of self and a genuine belief in your own self-worth and values. Set your boundaries in your head first. Forget about what other people tell you, and connect with what *you alone* think and feel is right.

Step Two: Gain further clarity

It is not enough to simply know that you have "boundary issues." What kinds of boundaries do you have issues with? With whom and in what context? What kind of issues are these and why are they happening?

The more clarity you have on yourself, the clearer and more defined your boundaries can be, and the better chance you have of people seeing and respecting them. May people with boundary issues spend so little time considering their own wants and limits that it may feel uncomfortable to delve too deeply into the details of their own needs, but it is necessary for every autonomous adult that wishes to take charge of their mental, emotional, and physical well-being.

Zoom in on exactly where your boundaries need to be established or tightened up (or, perhaps, even loosened). You may start with romantic relationships and look at the dynamic between you and your partner.

Where are there issues—in sexual, emotional, mental, or even financial boundaries? A mix of all of these? Even well-established relationships will need you to occasionally revisit old boundaries.

Decide what your deal breakers are and identify the areas you can compromise on. It's OK to have general, abstract boundaries, but can you also think of practical actions and events they apply to? The more specific, the better. Use your emotions and intuition to point you in the direction of areas that you feel unsafe, overwhelmed, disrespected, or unseen. Because you've made up your mind on your own beforehand, these should be easier to communicate with others.

Having frank discussions with your partner will sometimes entail you telling them, essentially, to back off, but also be sure to make room to confront anything that *you* do to allow your boundaries to be dismissed. It's not so important why they do something—it's more important why you allow it!

Is the problem that your boundaries aren't properly formed in your mind, or is the problem that you have trouble implementing them? Are you merely saying the words, but internally don't really believe them yourself? Are you unconsciously *hoping* that the other person will push past boundaries to show that they love or need you and are willing to take care of you and remove all of your responsibilities? These are tricky questions. Watch carefully if either you or the other person is making excuses for why your boundaries can't be respected. Take note. The better you can understand all the obstacles standing in your way, the sooner you can start to remove them.

Step Three: Seek support

Sometimes, with the difficult work of boundary setting, we can start to feel like the world is a hostile, complicated place. It feels like we have to build walls to keep out enemies—and it's so hard to decide who to trust in the first place! Even though boundary work is a necessarily personal activity, it doesn't mean that you can't get support from others as you go.

Testing out new limits, or even a new identity, can make you feel a little exposed and vulnerable. Why not get support as you work it out? A trusted family member, friend, or mental health professional can be a sounding board and an anchor that you can keep checking in with. It can take time to learn to trust and honor your own judgment, but there's nothing wrong with leaning on others temporarily while you figure it out.

Though establishing boundaries might feel like an "unworthy" reason to seek help, think of the amount of time—potentially years and decades—that you have spent struggling with your current problems while trying to tackle it on your own. With the help of another person, you can greatly accelerate the process of healing and living a healthier life.

More importantly, you may need some sound legal and financial advice if your boundaries are in this area. Know that there are laws to protect your rights and that there are experts in most areas who can give you neutral, trustworthy advice. The police can ensure your physical safety in the immediate moment, but a shelter, helpline, social worker, or nonprofit organization can give you the resources you need so that you don't feel alone. It can be very healing to share your vulnerabilities and goals with others who you can trust to respect and honor those boundaries.

Step Four: Plan your move

Some boundaries are set subtly and nonverbally. As you become better at boundaries, you may set them naturally and early on in your interactions with others, meaning you seldom have to put your foot down. Other boundary issues will require you to have a more direct (and, sometimes, awkward or difficult) conversation with the person who violated them. It's normal to feel anxious and guilty about doing this. So many of us have been socialized to never rock the boat or offend others—even if they've wronged us!

You can get through it if you prepare carefully. Beforehand, meditate or visualize so that you are in tune with how you feel. Be kind, patient, and accepting with yourself. Try not to approach others in a state of anger or fear—this will seldom get you what you want. Similarly, don't make it personal (because it really isn't). Rather, practice being calm. Tell yourself, "I can do this. I have a right to set my boundaries," and trust that asserting your worth does not hurt or offend others and is never something to feel guilty about. If you can speak from your heart and truly carry an unshakable sense of your own value, it will be easier to speak out clearly and be heard.

Similarly, if you're trying to loosen your overly rigid boundaries, the prospect of trusting others or allowing yourself to be vulnerable might be equally frightening. You might have been operating with your current boundaries long enough to be unable to imagine what it would be like not to have that wall of protection around you. In such cases, it is important to remember that stepping out of your comfort zone is the key to new and enriching experiences. Effective planning will help reduce any anxiety you have about this.

Step Five: Communicate properly

The best thing is to have boundary conversations well before there is any conflict or misunderstanding. However, if you have a history with someone and have set up a poor precedent already, you may need to broach the topic directly. Consider that people are *always* communicating with one another, only they do it unconsciously, nonverbally. When people violate boundaries, they are communicating something to you, and when you allow that violation, you are responding, too. Think of conscious verbal communication as merely a way of bringing unconscious dialogue out into the open, where you can claim it and speak openly.

Use "I" statements. These will remind you to talk from your own agency and responsibility. For example, nobody can "make" anyone feel anything. Rather, say, "When you did that, I felt this way" rather than, "You make me feel uncomfortable." Own your behavior and resist laying blame. Remember that you are not really trying to get anything from the other person, but instead communicating to them what you will do and how you will be in your subsequent interactions.

Avoid falling into victim mode, seeking contrition or apologies, or blaming. Stick to your own needs, values, and desires. Be clear about what you'd like from the other person going forward, but phrase this for what it is: a desire, not an order. Use a tone of voice and posture that communicates self-confidence, and drop "hedging language" like, "If you wouldn't mind...," "If that makes sense," or, "I'm so, so sorry, but maybe could you please...".

Importantly, acknowledge that the other person is free to respond exactly as they will. Your talk can have consequences—it could even end the relationship. But hopefully, you've spent time already ironing out your own needs and values, and you know that you are unwilling to be in a relationship where someone is uninterested in respecting you in the way you need to be respected. Don't backtrack or apologize.

Hold your head high and speak up—you don't need to be sheepish about talking candidly and maturely about your needs. If you show that your needs are important to you, others are more likely to treat them as important, too. Similarly, if they feel like they can get away with violating them, they will invariably try to do so.

Nevertheless, be prepared for resistance. Even if it's not the case, many people will assume that you are attacking or criticizing them, but don't see conflict or tension as a sign that you shouldn't be enforcing a boundary. You are deliberately changing the terms of your relationship, so give them time to process and respond as they need to, without rushing in to apologize or take responsibility or blame. They may be disappointed—that's natural. It's OK if they don't understand. It's OK if they don't agree. Neither of these things is required for you to stand your ground.

Sometimes, the hardest work will come later, when you are confronted with someone who deliberately tests your boundary again. This may be about control for them, their own unmet needs, or simple disrespect, but don't tolerate it. Follow through in the way you've already decided for yourself, and speak out clearly and calmly. "I've asked you repeatedly to please not smoke around me and my baby. Since you can't respect that boundary, I'm going to have to step away from this relationship."

Some other phrases you could experiment with are:

"If you continue to yell and call me names, I'm going to end this conversation."

"I'm happy to help, but I can longer babysit on the weekends, I'm afraid." (This is said without launching into excuses, explanations, or apologies. It is also said without needing to launch into finding a new solution to the babysitting problem for them.)

"I'm sorry you're going through a tough time right now, but I'm not the right person to help."

"I'm so glad you invited me, but I'm going to have to sit this one out!"

"Please don't do that again, it makes me uncomfortable."

"That's very kind, thank you, but no." (This is said to turn down offers of food, alcohol, or inappropriate gifts.)

"No." (This is perfect on its own!)

When you're choosing your phrasing, make sure to include an actual request, intention, or limit. State how you feel, how the other person's actions are affecting you, and, if appropriate, explain your values and desires in the situation. You need to clearly state what you want or don't want to happen. State clearly what the consequences are. Otherwise, you risk merely making a complaint or venting, leaving the other person aware that you're unhappy with them, but unsure of what that really means.

People may try to guilt-trip you but remember that you will not be forced into anything and you are not forcing anyone else into anything—you are merely outlining the reasonable conditions of being in a relationship with you. If someone shows that they are unwilling to respect this, then, in effect, it is *they* who have ended the relationship and not you. You have merely followed through.

The stronger the resistance to a healthy boundary, the more evidence you have that it was needed in the first place—stand your ground. The fallout of setting up stronger boundaries (especially if you have a history as a bit of a doormat) can be large. But try to remember that any connections or people you lose were only those connections and people that disrespected your happiness and well-being. If you think of it this way, you haven't lost anything truly valuable. The amount of love and support you had before dropping a disrespectful friend is the same as you have after dropping them!

Step Six: Follow through

You've made your request. You've held the other person accountable. Now what? After you've communicated a boundary, pause and assess how it went. Did you follow through according to your strategy? How well did it work and what can you improve on next time? The great thing about boundary setting is that it only becomes easier the more practice you get. While it may feel scary to assert yourself at first, you'll soon experience the magic power of "no" as a wonderfully liberating tool. It reduces your anxiety, empowers you, and brings the things you care about into clear focus, while letting harmful or irrelevant things drift away from your attention.

Going forward, pay attention so that you can catch small boundary violations early on, before they become bigger ones. It's much easier! Likewise, you may like to start with a relatively strict boundary and negotiate it down, rather than state a boundary that is already a compromise for you, especially if you have a history of acquiescing under pressure. If you can hold your nerve and trust your judgment, refusing to be pushed or bullied or talked out of your boundaries, a wonderful thing happens: you start to realize that you *are* in control of your experiences. You *can* decide who and what to permit into your world. Notice and relish this feeling when it arises. This is the satisfaction of knowing that you are living with integrity and respect for your own values. Well done!

For some of us, setting a boundary and actually following through with a consequence can be eye-opening and something we might never have done before. Once you realize and truly understand your power to do this, the next time it will be easier, and eventually, it will soon feel natural. In time, you'll restore your inbuilt ability to protect, maintain, and love who you are.

Common Missteps

What characterizes most of the steps and tips we've covered so far is this: a focus on *you*, your wants, and your limits, rather than on others and what they need and want from you. Chronic people-pleasers are not used to turning this attention and concern onto themselves, but they need to if they hope to heal broken boundaries that open them to invasion from others.

Sometimes, an attempt to set a boundary can fail. Maybe you feel guilty and backpedal, apologizing for ruffling any feathers. Maybe you allow yourself to be bullied back into line because it's less scary than having to stand your ground. Or, maybe, you immediately follow your boundary with a promise or consolation of some kind to "make up" for the fact that you said no—landing yourself at square one again.

Proper boundaries take time to build, but as you learn, try be patient with yourself. If it didn't work as you expected, gently ask yourself why and try again. Growth takes patience and courage. The following are the most common mistakes people looking to set healthy boundaries fall prey to, and how to avoid them.

Mistake 1: You are aggressive and not assertive

Have you ever suppressed your rage and anger to such a degree that when it did finally come out, people were completely caught off guard by your seemingly disproportionate blow-up? While understandable, this is not a responsible way to set boundaries. You never have to be mean, hurtful, unkind, or judgmental to set a boundary. In fact, if a boundary looks like it's merely you lashing out, people are less likely to take it seriously. If you're upset or mad, wait until you're calm to have any discussions.

Though it is natural to be angry when someone violates your boundaries, especially if it has happened repeatedly, a good way to tone down the aggression is this. As far as you possibly can, do not assume malice on the part of the offender. Their actions likely stem from ignorance born out of their own personal history.

Granted, some with narcissistic and abusive personalities will actively hurt you out of bad intentions, but being aggressive in response ultimately won't help you achieve your goal. Use a firm tone when needed, but never scream, insult, or demean.

Mistake 2: Centering the other person's emotions and not your own

Repeat to yourself as often as necessary: you are not responsible for the emotions of others. When setting a boundary, keep the focus squarely on your emotions, needs, and limits. This is all you can really claim responsibility for, anyway. You don't have to take care of someone's disappointment, apologize, feel bad that you've upset them, or anything else.

You don't have to wring your hangs and act pained and full of remorse—own your boundary and state it without drama and contrition. How the other person responds to that is strictly their business. You can, of course, say things like, "I'm sorry you feel that way," or, "I can see that you're not happy about that," but stop there. You don't need to rush in to soothe them, solve their problems, or take on a dose of blame and guilt.

Mistake 3: Poor timing

Poor timing can ruin things, even if you do everything else correctly. You can use the right tone, posture, words, and as many "I" statements as you want, but it is also imperative that you choose the right moment to convey any frustrations you have.

It comes down to planning again. While it's certainly a good idea to defend a boundary the moment it's crossed, it's better to establish your limits preemptively, when you are both calm and receptive. Pick a time when you both can talk privately without being rushed, and wait till you are able to speak calmly and firmly.

It might also help to give the other person a chance to decide the time of your conversation. Simply approach them and convey that you need to talk to them and you would appreciate it if they informed you when they are free to do so. This gives them a sense of control over the situation that is lost when you don't give them adequate notice.

Following this step will clearly indicate to them that the topic of the conversation is of a serious nature, giving them the time and space to prepare for it mentally.

Once you've stated your intention, it's OK to let the other person process at their own pace. If there's no need to have a drawn-out, angst-filled dialogue, don't. Sometimes, people might have an immediate negative reaction to perceived criticism, but realize their mistake later. Give them the time to right any wrongs they might commit in your conversation.

Mistake 4: Ramping up the drama

All this talk of confrontation and planning a conversation can sound rather serious. In truth, it's all about making sure that you're in the right headspace as you navigate territory you may be uncomfortable with. In real life, most everyday conflicts and disagreements can be solved simply and directly. There's no need for angsty, over-the-top conversations that go on for ages.

If your intention is clear, you should be able to communicate fairly effectively in very little time. Stick to the point and be concise. You may dilute your message by adding in too much detail or explanation. The other person doesn't need to know all about your personal emotional journey on the road to self-esteem, or why you've arrived at this particular boundary, or the insights you've had about your childhood. All you need to tell them is your boundary—and a good boundary is short, sweet, and *very* clear.

If you are unsure of the correct way to express yourself, don't spend too much time fretting over it. This will increase the likelihood of you not following through, or letting the issue fester for too long to appropriately object to it later. If someone wrongs you, it is advisable to not take too long to approach them about it. You can just express your boundary and an I statement about how its violation made you feel to get your message across in a timely manner.

Mistake 5: Shutting down dialogue

A boundary doesn't have to be mean or harsh. Just because you are setting a limit, it doesn't mean that you are closing off the conversation, terminating the relationship, or making any final conclusions about the entire relationship (unless you are, in which case, you'll have to say so).

If your boundaries are intact and clear, it's OK to talk things through with the other person. They might like to explain their side of the story, to apologize, to clarify, or ask you questions.

Welcome this dialogue if it's well-meaning. While you certainly don't owe anyone an explanation, it goes a long way to show that you are, in fact, open to dialogue. Be careful if you suspect that you may be being talked down or manipulated. But people who have unwittingly violated a boundary may well want to discuss how that happened, defend themselves, and perhaps even share some of their own concerns. Boundaries are there not to shut down relationships, but to allow for better ones.

Show good faith by talking honestly about how you'd like the dynamic to change, as appropriate. That said, if you're dealing with a truly awful person who has no intention of seeing things from your point of view, remember that you have one more option up your sleeve: just walk away. Forever.

Dealing with Repeat Offenders

The good people in your life will happily respect and work with your boundaries. They may even celebrate them, glad that you're taking care of yourself. The bad people? Not so much. It's a skill to set up boundaries in the ordinary world of demands and intrusions, but it's an art to set up boundaries when you've had the misfortune of dealing with someone who refuses to take your agency and well-being into consideration.

We know we need to "stand our ground" and "be assertive," but it's not always clear what that looks like in the moment, especially since some exploitative people don't magically disappear just because we've started to love ourselves more!

Ordinary people may inadvertently step over our boundaries (as we might do), but will generally respond well when we assert them. This section is for those people who *don't* respond well to and respect a boundary. Sadly, there are no magical incantations or special tricks that will banish such people from your life. Rather, you protect yourself using all of the same principles and techniques already explored so far—except, for truly toxic people, firm boundaries matter more than ever. Thank life in its infinite wisdom for sending you challenging people who force you to really dig deep and set up rock-solid boundaries!

Realize that everything that happens before and after the boundary is set almost matter more—are you regularly practicing self-care? Are you working towards a healthy self-love, recognizing and taking care of your own needs? Eating well, sleeping enough, and exercising strengthen the physical body against attack, and self-care strengthens the emotional and spiritual immune system from attack in the same way. So, keep in tip-top condition. Regularly journal, ask for help, and rethink your boundaries, needs, and values. Say "no" and don't feel guilty. Finally, anticipate that you will get resistance from some people. Understand what this resistance is and you ensure that you're not thrown by it.

When anyone resists your boundary, understand that it is essentially them telling you, "I don't agree that you are worth better treatment than what I'm willing to give you." Think about that. Though they may use all kinds of manipulation tactics that may distract and confuse you, the underlying message is always the same. You have requested to be respected and honored, and the other person has clearly told you "no."

Exactly *how* you respond to every boundary violator in every circumstance will vary. But whatever you do, it needs to be an affirmation of your right to have a boundary, and your following through according to your own belief in your self-worth. People can resist your boundaries in a thousand different ways, but there's no need to get bogged down in understanding the details of their resistance—only notice its existence.

People may not really listen or take the time to actually hear what you are saying to them. They may go into defense mode and assume that you're attacking them, starting a fight, or placing blame (usually, this is because they feel somewhat guilty and know unconsciously that they are in the wrong!). They may turn things around and try to paint you as the difficult, fussy, or overly sensitive one for holding people accountable. They may try to make you feel bad for being mean to them (i.e. withholding something that they feel entitled to) or try to insinuate that you are being selfish, unrealistic, or unfair.

They may make a *big* show of how sad, uncomfortable, or inconvenienced they are by your boundary, playing up their victim status or acting mortally offended (you would see how quickly this act would vanish the moment you capitulated, however!). They may deny that what they've done is wrong at all, implying that your assessment of the situation is wrong or irrelevant. They may claim that the event or situation never even happened. They may turn passive aggressive and say "fine," leaving you to wonder what underhanded revenge they're cooking up for you later.

They may make you promise something else to them since you've so clearly failed to do what they want in this instance. They may even threaten to invoke a higher power—call the police, tell the boss on you, tattle to your mother, or even call into question your faith, your intelligence, your commitment, your sanity, your worth as a human being…

Here's the secret: none of this matters. The above forms of resistance will take any shape they need to in order to try and get you to do what they want. That's their only function, and it's got nothing to do with you. You do not need to engage with manipulation. You do not need to understand it. By setting a boundary, you are not instantly making yourself responsible for that person's life. Try to listen well below the resistance, and you will hear the same old message again and again: "I don't agree that you are worth better treatment than what I'm willing to give you." Respond to that hidden message and none of the manipulation tactics will work.

Tips for Nonnegotiable Boundaries with Toxic People

- Realize that you may have to say "no" more than once. Know that this doesn't mean you're doing anything wrong—rather, it proves how necessary the boundary is. You may need to *constantly* maintain and defend your boundaries with certain people. However, if you feel exhausted by having to enforce boundaries with someone and

repeated reminders don't work, it might be better to simply walk away from the relationship.
- Prepare for and anticipate resistance. If you know beforehand how you will respond, you'll go into any interaction feeling focused and empowered.
- It's always OK to physically leave a situation you feel threatened in. Don't worry about appearing polite—just leave.
- Decline invitations, refuse to answer calls, or simply walk away if you're facing someone who repeatedly tries to push your buttons. If a third person is pressuring you to do these things, you might want to consider distancing yourself from them, too.
- Keep contact very minimal or cut it completely, if possible. Change phone numbers, travel a different route to avoid meeting them, or block them on social media.
- You don't need to gain any "closure" or to explain why you're taking a step back—just do it. Guard against

secretly hoping that flouncing off will have the other person rushing towards you again. They are not likely to suddenly care about your needs, and if they were the kind of person who needed the threat of you leaving to consider treating you well, this tells you everything you need to know.

- If it's an abusive or dangerous situation, make sure that others are aware of what's happening, document what you can, and seek help, advice, and support from others willing to help you.
- If the person is a family member, colleague, or someone you can't reasonably avoid, try the "grey rock" technique: you can be present but disengage, disconnect, and be, emotionally, like a grey rock (i.e. someone who can't be manipulated!). Give boring answers, don't rise to the bait of drama, avoid eye contact, and keep interactions as short as possible. Don't feed into manipulation. Simply say "uh-huh"

and shift your attention. Keep things polite, neutral, boring, and impersonal. The less interesting and remarkable your engagement, the less there is for a narcissist, abuser, or boundary-crosser to work with!

When people repeatedly break your boundaries and communicate loudly and clearly that they have no intention of respecting them, *believe them*. There hasn't been a miscommunication—they simply don't care. You don't have to "make nice." Rather, treat a person with a known propensity to disregard your boundaries as you would anyone else who insulted you: ignore it and remove yourself as quickly as possible.

For situations that move beyond the realm of boundaries and into the realm of outright abuse, you need to dig your heels in deeper. Your boundaries will step in to protect you, but you will also need other kinds of barriers around you, be they legal or financial. Seek help from women's shelters, a mental health professional, a social worker, a spiritual teacher, trusted family members, or friends. Don't be afraid to speak out and say what is happening.

Serious abuse can, in a strange way, force some people to take a long hard look at themselves and what they absolutely aren't willing to tolerate, ever, from anyone. Though painful, this can be an empowering and clarifying moment. If you're trying to extricate yourself from an abusive situation, use any anger and pain you feel to protect yourself. However difficult it may seem in the moment, you can and will come out the other end!

Summary:

- Creating and maintaining healthy boundaries is not something we can manage to do overnight. Old habits die hard, and we must work towards building boundaries that we are comfortable with. Though it is completely up to us what we deem to be a boundary, there are some steps we can follow to make the process simpler.
- To start, it is crucial for us to gain clarity regarding what our

boundaries really are. We need to articulate for ourselves hard limits that we aren't willing to tolerate, and the boundaries that we might be willing to compromise on from time to time. Survey your current relationships or friendships and identify boundaries that need strengthening or change. Ascertain them by category and try to identify the cause of the poor state of any boundaries in each relationship. Once you've done this, communicate your boundaries respectfully by using "I" statements and stand your ground when you're met with resistance. If you need support, seek help from a professional.

- It is obvious that we will make mistakes in our attempts to build healthy boundaries. However, knowing some of the common ones might help you avoid them. These include being too aggressive, not being mindful of your timing, being overly concerned with the emotions of others at the expense of your own,

and being too dramatic by having long, drawn-out conversations. Remember that all you need to do is communicate a boundary using "I" statements.
- Unfortunately, some people will continue to disrespect your boundaries despite being warned repeatedly. In such cases, you might have to cut contact either temporarily or permanently, even if these are people who you value and love dearly. By refusing to respect your boundaries, they are essentially telling you that your well-being does not matter to them. These are not the kinds of people you need in your life, anyway, and letting them go can often be the easiest and best option.

Chapter Six: It's Not Your Turn

In this book, we've mostly considered all of the ways that boundaries can be too weak or too porous. We've also seen that boundary issues of this kind often stem from early childhood experiences that taught us faulty beliefs about the healthy way to love, connect, communicate, and be with others while maintaining a personal identity.

But we've also seen that no man is an island, and that boundary problems are a relational issue, pointing to the pattern of behavior and engagement we have with others—in other words, it takes two to tango. It may well be that you are a chronic people-pleaser whose sense of self is constantly invaded by others. But far more likely is that you exist in a complex network of maladaptive boundaries, where your boundary issue is really much bigger than yourself. Think of the boundary between the sand and the water on the shoreline—is it the beginning of the beach sand or the end of the ocean? Can one change the boundary without it affecting the other?

As human beings, we exist in social groups and derive much of our identity from one another. We share boundaries and, like the shoreline, these lines may well shift over time according to the needs of both. As you become more aware of your boundaries and better at understanding your own needs, you can head back into the world with a more nuanced understanding of your place in the great fabric of human connectedness.

In dysfunctional family relationships, it can be hard to determine whose pain is whose, who is responsible for what. The lines are blurred. As you improve these, however, you're not only doing work on your own self-identity and values, but at the same time you are also saying something about the relationships you have with the people you share that boundary with. By changing the terms of engagement, you make it easier for the right people to connect with you, and make less room for the wrong people.

An underappreciated part of fixing boundary issues is turning the problem around and asking from the other side of the boundary. Do *you* ever violate other people's boundaries? Everyone is keen to blow the whistle when they have been wronged, but fewer people ask how they may be wronging others. A young man's mother might be particularly smothering, for example, putting her nose in all of his affairs and saying, "You can't move out. Who will take care of me?" to guilt him out of his growing independence. But at the same time, the young man may be consciously or unconsciously taking advantage of his mother financially. There are many boundary violations here and they go *both ways*. Both mother and son have failed to set up healthy adult boundaries and take responsibility for themselves, but at the same time, both are intruding into the other's world far more than is healthy.

In real life, things can get very complicated, and it's seldom as simple as identifying the villain and the victim. Sometimes, the victim is complicit in their victimhood, and were, in fact, the first to victimize themselves. Sometimes, the victim and villain swap roles endlessly. Sometimes, the victim in one context is the villain later on in another context. In other words, if you have issues with people breaking your boundaries, you may also have issues with breaking theirs.

Naturally, we don't like to think of ourselves as mean boundary-pushers, but there are many subtle ways to push a boundary that you may not have thought of:

- Someone is upset or angry and you hug them, even though they clearly don't want you to. You think it's sweet and cute, but they may feel violated.
- Giving unsolicited advice, even and especially if you're "just trying to help."

- Sharing a secret with someone when you've promised someone else to keep it—this violates two people's boundaries at once.
- Taking up people's time by overstaying, demanding long conversations when they're busy, calling late at night, etc. On the other hand, being late or canceling at the last minute has a similar effect.
- Oversharing details of your life without thinking about if the other person wants to or can handle it. Sharing personal and intimate details can feel like "opening up" and being candid, but it can also put the other person on the spot.
- Gossiping.
- Interrupting people when they talk.
- Swooping in to solve someone's problem for them without asking them if that's what they want (another case of "I was only trying to help…").
- Trying to force someone to be a part of your healing process, confused as to why they don't seem to be

interested in hearing your confessions.
- Being condescending or acting like your worldview is the only correct one, "explaining" things to others or offering help that is really just an insult ("I see you got a new haircut! You should have asked me for the number for my hairdresser!").

As you can see, boundary violations are not just about being an abusive jerk or very obviously insulting or hurting someone. The fact is, we've all probably overstepped the mark at some point or another. Part of learning about our own boundaries entails becoming more sensitive to and able to detect the boundaries of others. Respect is a reciprocal thing—the more we respect ourselves, the easier it is for us to respect others.

When you consider other people fully, you start to get a three-dimensional picture of exactly why boundaries are so important: they help us stay connected to one another in optimal ways, serving and helping one another, but also staying separate enough to maintain our agency, free will, and unique identities.

Negotiating boundaries is a lifetime's work, but it's always a balancing act between your boundaries and everyone else's (yes, they are entitled to them just as you are to yours!). It's a balance between self-respect and respect for others, between your needs and theirs. It's a constant dance between self and other, between give and take. If we manage it right, we get to be fulfilled and autonomous individuals and enjoy closeness *and* intimacy with others. Get it wrong and we enjoy neither.

Mutual respect and acknowledgment is like understanding that the shoreline belongs both to the ocean and to the beach. There are always ways for compassionate, conscious people to meet their different needs together. The healthy boundary is the one that helps you find that way.

Boundaries are not either/or. If only one person benefits, it's not a good boundary. Rather, good boundaries are and/and.

You matter AND they matter.

You have needs AND they have needs.

You get what you want AND they get what they want.

You want to be close to others AND you want to be separate.

Cautiously Prioritizing Others Again

- Remember, there is no rule book. If someone states a boundary, accept it. You don't have to approve it, understand it, endorse it, or share it as your own. It's *theirs*. Become curious what their boundary means to them, rather than trying to verify it or decide whether it's "right" or whether they're allowed to have it.
- Respect uniqueness. Try to honor that every person you meet has different ideas, thoughts, longings, fears, beliefs, and values, and that all of these are not threats to you.
- Learn to listen. Forget about yourself for a moment and simply become curious about what it's like to be the

other person—don't see their world through your eyes, see their world through *their* eyes. What are their needs? What do they value and why?
- Don't assume. Other people's perceptions, preferences, and interpretations may be very different from yours. They're not wrong, just different. Can you understand this difference rather than trying to control it?
- Pay attention to verbal and nonverbal cues. Err on the side of caution and wait to be invited in closer, or else ask permission before taking a step. Subtle body language, as well as changes in voice and eye contact, can let you know if your advances are welcome or not.
- Be aware that some people may come from very different cultural backgrounds or have profoundly different experiences (think about those with autism, language barriers, learning and developmental disorders, speech impediments, or mental health issues). Practice extra

tact since you cannot assume what will be welcome and what won't be. When in doubt, you can always respectfully ask.

If you find yourself stepping over barriers a little too often, try to understand what is compelling you to do so. Do you have a misplaced need to "help" others? Think about whether this is really a control issue, which is, in itself, nothing more than fear.

People who invade the boundaries of others may have faulty beliefs about intimacy and how they can win love, respect, or attention from others. You may have grown up in a household where you were frequently blamed for other people's problems—but you also enjoyed the dubious honor of being able to blame them the next day for yours! This may have convinced you that a loving relationship is a trade, or two people mutually keeping one another hostage—"I allow you to use me if I get to use you." If this sounds familiar, you may need to work on how to find intimacy with people while still respecting their individuality.

As you learn to say "no," you may become more and more comfortable with other people doing the same. This doesn't threaten the closeness between you—in fact, it strengthens it.

The ultimate marker of a close relationship is when both of you are comfortable expressing any issues you might have with each other and both can expect a peaceful resolution to them. It's OK to compromise a little to find that healthy balance between your needs and someone else's—all relationships are give-and-take. But make sure it's truly balanced, i.e. you can give help when it's wanted, and you can accept help when you need it. You can demand respect, but also know how to give it. You are entitled to people honoring your boundaries, and you are also happy to honor other people's.

Healthy boundaries are not something we merely tack onto a finished and completed life, like building a fence around a forest. Rather, boundaries emerge naturally and organically from the way we are and the beliefs we hold about ourselves. They are an expression of everything we are. Our boundaries can be thought of as the tools we use to negotiate meaningful and respectful connections with others—when our external relationships aren't healthy, it's because our internal ones aren't, either.

When we heal our boundaries, we are really healing our own sense of self-worth and our identity. We are digging deep to understand what we can give to this world and what we'd like to receive from it. If this balance is healthy, we can set ourselves up to live in a state of happy, dynamic equilibrium. Within ourselves and with our dealings with others, we can take steps to make the lines between us and the world clearer, more conscious, and better able to serve us and our unique needs.

The perfect boundary is a paradox: in knowing ourselves deeply, we allow ourselves to more deeply know others; in strengthening and defending our vulnerability, we practice trusting others; by putting ourselves first, we understand what it means to be selfless. In drawing a bright, clear line between two things, we magically make it so much easier for them to be together.

Living a life with healthy boundaries takes a lifetime of work because we are constantly learning things about ourselves and others. We also change as people, prioritize different things over time, and grasp new and better ways to communicate in our social interactions. It can be daunting to have this responsibility thrust upon you.

Recognizing that you are in control of most, if not all, outcomes that you experience on a day-to-day basis is a monumental task for someone who hasn't done so already. Yet, once we learn the right way to go about setting and enforcing boundaries, it makes us truly free to determine our fate and happiness for ourselves.

Takeaways

- So far, we have primarily focused on the way others violate our boundaries. However, we also inevitably violate boundaries that others have. This does not necessarily make us toxic or bad individuals, but it helps to recognize our faulty behavioral patterns so that we can fix them and have healthier relationships. Identifying our own mistakes can be hard, but some examples of pushing others' boundaries might be engaging in gossip, arriving excessively late to a meeting, sharing secrets with others despite being told not to, etc.

- Even if we find that we have been less than pleasant in some of our interactions, there are several things we can do to better ourselves. The first and most important step here is to accept and listen when others tell us about any misdeed we may have committed. Just like we are free to have boundaries based on our values and desires, so are others. There is no right or wrong boundary, and we must be accommodating of others without judgement. In cases of deep cultural differences, it is important to remember that the other person comes from a completely different

background, with unique experiences that are different from our own. Generally, it always pays to be compassionate and willing to talk it out with others.
- Ultimately, maintaining healthy boundaries is a task that we have to persist with throughout our lives. As we discover new and better ways to communicate, develop new values and priorities, or enter relationships with different sets of people, the way we enforce our boundaries must adapt. Though maintaining healthy boundaries can sometimes come with conflict and unpleasantness, the many benefits outweigh these minor cons.

Summary Guide

Chapter One: The Line in the Sand
- A boundary is a line between us as individuals and the rest of the world. Inside of this boundary lies everything related to ourselves, things that are relevant to us and that are under our control. Outside of it is everything else.
- In our social interactions, our boundaries define what we are comfortable with, based on our values and conceptions of what is important and what isn't. Having healthy boundaries is a key component of good relationships and friendships.
- It is common for people to have poor boundaries due to the cultural messages or upbringing that they have experienced. We are repeatedly told to avoid saying "no" in our lives, to quietly accept any mistreatment from others so as to not bother

anyone else. However, poor boundaries result in low self-esteem, a sense of being out of control of your life, and resentment towards others. It also leads to us being subjected to exploitative behavior from those who are all too happy to use our poor boundaries to their advantage.
- There are several different types of boundaries that one can have. These include physical, emotional, spiritual, sexual, digital, time, and even energy boundaries. All of these various categories, however, reinforce the same message—that you are important and deserve to be respected. Whether this is with respect to your body, your feelings, your time, your sexual preferences, or something else, you have a right to demand what you desire in an appropriate manner.
- This book and the following chapters are for those who, for one reason or another, have come to develop boundaries that are either too loose or too rigid. This requires not only

being familiar with what exactly healthy boundaries are, but also a fundamental shift in how you view yourself.

Chapter Two: Your Relationship with Boundaries

- Personal boundaries are limits we place for ourselves and others in our interactions with others. They define the kinds of behavior that we are both comfortable and not comfortable with. However, the process of setting up boundaries can go awry if we choose boundaries that are either too harsh or too permeable. For instance, rejecting intimacy altogether is a sign of the former, while being too afraid to speak up for yourself is an example of the latter.
- Asserting your boundaries can be a frightening and scary prospect, especially for those of us who have never done so before. We may be afraid of conflict, or terrified at the possibility of being disliked by others

who might not agree with our boundaries. Despite the initial reluctance, it is nevertheless crucial for us to express and communicate with others things that are not acceptable to us. This helps us to develop a positive self-esteem and attract healthy relationships in our lives.

- We tend to think that boundaries make us selfish, that we won't be well-liked by others if we enforce them, or that it is somehow overly demanding of others. None of these are true. Learning how to create and maintain boundaries is an important skill that is useful for everyone.
- There are many different reasons why so many of us have poor boundaries to begin with. One of the most common ones is suffering from childhood trauma, as this is where beliefs are formulated and solidified, for better or worse. Children who did not feel safe growing up or had their boundaries routinely violated are bound to internalize the lack of self-

worth that others have projected onto them. Our cultures in general also tend to valorize sacrifice and martyrdom at the expense of personal happiness. Though we may have been disadvantaged in terms of learning about boundaries, it is nevertheless important to recognize that enforcing and communicating boundaries is solely our responsibility.

Chapter Three: Boundaries: The Strong, Weak, Good, and Bad

- It is all too easy to fall into the trap of replacing loose boundaries with ones that are overly rigid. We might feel like we are protecting ourselves by erecting a huge emotional wall around us, but in truth, we are simply insulating ourselves from positive experiences that are necessary to live a fulfilling life. As such, we must discover the mean that lies between these two types of boundaries. Those

are the ones that we should aim to integrate into our daily lives.
- Boundaries that are too weak will inevitably be an emotional drain on our mental health. When we keep such boundaries, we implicitly allow others to trample over us. This leads to us feeling used, unappreciated, and taken for granted. On the other hand, rigid boundaries can make us feel extremely lonely. It is understandable to be defensive and overprotective if we have been betrayed or hurt by those closest to us, but keeping everyone at an arm's length only leaves us feeling alone and uncared for.
- The key to setting good boundaries is to focus on what feels comfortable to *you*, and nobody else. It can be tempting to look up and simply copy the kind of boundaries we think we *should* have, but ultimately, if we want to live a free life, we have to live by our own rules. This doesn't mean that we never compromise or be flexible. Negotiating interactions

always involves some give-and-take. The important thing here is that the giving and taking are something that we both consent to and are willing to accept.
- All great romantic relationships are based on healthy boundaries set up by both parties. Even if you're starting from a place of low self-worth, with some perseverance, you, too, can be the type of person who naturally has healthy boundaries in relationships.

Chapter Four: Knowing Thyself
- Your identity and relationship with boundaries are inextricably linked. Those with poor boundaries often struggle with them because they have never truly reflected upon what it is that they want. On the other hand, rigid boundaries are a sign of fear and insecurity about the world and its potential for causing pain to us. Our identity forms the basis for our values, and our values are instrumental to our boundaries. Only

by cultivating an awareness of what our values are can we start to build healthy boundaries.

- We live in a world where everyone has boundaries, strong or weak. As such, we must be mindful of not only our own boundaries, but also those of the ones around us. If someone has overly rigid boundaries, they might end up stepping over our own. Alternatively, if we have loose boundaries, we might be subjected to abuse from those who enjoy controlling us for their own benefit. Anyone who repeatedly violates our boundaries despite being warned is likely being abusive, and must be dealt with appropriately.
- "I" statements are an invaluable tool when it comes to communicating your boundaries to others. These statements aim to convey how particular actions committed by others make us feel. If, say, we are annoyed by our spouse not doing their share of chores, we might tell

them "I feel anxious and taken for granted when you...".
- Sometimes, simply communicating your boundaries to others will not persuade them to stop violating them. In such cases, it might help to ask ourselves some questions regarding this person. Is there any wiggle room with respect to your boundaries? Is there a pattern of any type of behavior that you can discern? Is this person even capable or willing to accept your boundaries? Are you allowing or enabling the violation of your boundaries in some way? Considering the answers to questions like these can help you determine the appropriate course of action when it comes to boundary violations.

Chapter Five: Boundaries, Brick by Brick
- Creating and maintaining healthy boundaries is not something we can manage to do overnight. Old habits die hard, and we must work towards

building boundaries that we are comfortable with. Though it is completely up to us what we deem to be a boundary, there are some steps we can follow to make the process simpler.

- To start, it is crucial for us to gain clarity regarding what our boundaries really are. We need to articulate for ourselves hard limits that we aren't willing to tolerate, and the boundaries that we might be willing to compromise on from time to time. Survey your current relationships or friendships and identify boundaries that need strengthening or change. Ascertain them by category and try to identify the cause of the poor state of any boundaries in each relationship. Once you've done this, communicate your boundaries respectfully by using "I" statements and stand your ground when you're met with resistance. If you need support, seek help from a professional.

- It is obvious that we will make mistakes in our attempts to build healthy boundaries. However, knowing some of the common ones might help you avoid them. These include being too aggressive, not being mindful of your timing, being overly concerned with the emotions of others at the expense of your own, and being too dramatic by having long, drawn-out conversations. Remember that all you need to do is communicate a boundary using "I" statements.
- Unfortunately, some people will continue to disrespect your boundaries despite being warned repeatedly. In such cases, you might have to cut contact either temporarily or permanently, even if these are people who you value and love dearly. By refusing to respect your boundaries, they are essentially telling you that your well-being does not matter to them. These are not the kinds of people you need in your life,

anyway, and letting them go can often be the easiest and best option.

Chapter Six: It's Not Your Turn

- So far, we have primarily focused on the way others violate our boundaries. However, we also inevitably violate boundaries that others have. This does not necessarily make us toxic or bad individuals, but it helps to recognize our faulty behavioral patterns so that we can fix them and have healthier relationships. Identifying our own mistakes can be hard, but some examples of pushing others' boundaries might be engaging in gossip, arriving excessively late to a meeting, sharing secrets with others despite being told not to, etc.
- Even if we find that we have been less than pleasant in some of our interactions, there are several things we can do to better ourselves. The first and most important step here is to accept and listen when others tell

us about any misdeed we may have committed. Just like we are free to have boundaries based on our values and desires, so are others. There is no right or wrong boundary, and we must be accommodating of others without judgement. In cases of deep cultural differences, it is important to remember that the other person comes from a completely different background, with unique experiences that are different from our own. Generally, it always pays to be compassionate and willing to talk it out with others.

- Ultimately, maintaining healthy boundaries is a task that we have to persist with throughout our lives. As we discover new and better ways to communicate, develop new values and priorities, or enter relationships with different sets of people, the way we enforce our boundaries must adapt. Though maintaining healthy boundaries can sometimes come with conflict and unpleasantness, the many benefits outweigh these minor cons.

www.ingramcontent.com/pod-product-compliance
Lightning Source LLC
Chambersburg PA
CBHW071342080526
44587CB00017B/2935